"*Conversations at the Girlville Diner* fed my soul, strengthened my faith, and tickled my funny bone. I can't wait to share this book with my friends."—**Annie Chapman,** *Christian artist, conference speaker, and author*

"*Delightful, genuine,* and *real* describe *Conversations at the Girlville Diner.* Kim and Chris have hit a triple off the wall . . . no, make that a homer. Enjoy a meal from their diner. You'll be glad you did!"—**Dennis "The Swan" Swanberg,** *"America's Minister of Encouragement," television host of* Swan's Place, *speaker, entertainer, and author*

"Kim and Chris are warm and witty, poignant and profound, spontaneous and spiritual! This book has left me deeply grateful to a God who lives so majestically and yet so personally through two very human women. I *highly recommend* this book to any woman who looks for the spiritual in the mundane things of life!"—**Mikki Peterson**, *Pastoral Staff/Women's Ministries, Willow Creek Community Church*

"This is like no diner I've ever been to. Kim and Chris have cooked up something absolutely refreshing and delicious. There's something for everyone here: humor-filled stories about faith, relationships, family, and the various quirky details of everyday life."—**Jackie Mitchum Yockey,** *Senior Talent Coordinator,* The 700 Club

D1401572

(Continued on back)

"Girlfriend chats. Funny stories. A reminder that God is still in control—no matter how crazy life gets. This book is for everyone who needs a laugh and a renewed perspective on life!"—**Jaye Martin,** *HeartCall Women's Evangelism, North American Mission Board*

"Delightfully real! Refreshingly transparent! Life applications grab you before you know it. Kim and Chris leave you hungry for more!"—**Carol Bryant,** *Director, Women's Ministries, Christ Church*

"*Conversations* is a feast for the soul. I laughed; I cried. This is definitely one diner I'll return to again and again."—**Kay DeKalb Smith,** *Christian entertainer, singer, comedian, known as "The Carol Burnett of Christian Comedy"*

"If spiritual wit is art, this book belongs in the Louvre."—**Dr. Gary B. Arnold,** *Educator*

"Like an afternoon chat with a special girlfriend, *Conversations* brings roars of laughter and tears of conviction. Its lighthearted yet perceptive look at the mundane pierces the heart with powerful spiritual truths."—**Dr. Robin J. Kohl,** *Educational consultant, lecturer*

"I always knew diners was the meetin' place where thangs—big thangs—happened. And I ain't a bit surprised The Big Guy Himself shows up on a regl'ar basis. I always knew my cookin' was deeevine." — **Lou "Doc" Schmedlapp,** *Proprietor and short order cook, Lucky Lou's Diner*

Conversations at the Girlville Diner

CONVERSATIONS AT

The GIRLVILLE Diner

KIM BOLTON *And* CHRIS WAVE

Finding God in the Hairdos & the Hash Browns

HAROLD
SHAW
PUBLISHERS

Several pieces have been previously published and appear in this book in different form: "The Naked Man" and "Pitfalls and Absurdities" in *Woman to Woman* and "Kendra," "Kiwi in Mouse Clothing," and "Love Soup" in *Tapestry*.

Some Scripture verses have not been put into quote marks because they are paraphrased by the authors.

Scripture quotations marked NIV are taken from the HOLY BIBLE, NEW INTERNATIONAL VERSION®. NIV® Copyright © 1973, 1978, 1984 International Bible Society. Used by permission of Zondervan Publishing House. All rights reserved.

Scripture quotations marked NASB taken from the *New American Standard Bible,* © 1960, 1962, 1963, 1968, 1971, 1972, 1973, 1975, 1977 by The Lockman Foundation. Used by permission.

ISBN 0-87788-171-5

Cover design by David LaPlaca

Interior design and typesetting by Carol Barnstable

Library of Congress Cataloging-in-Publication Data

Bolton, Kim, 1958-
    Conversations at the Girlville diner : finding God in the hairdos
and the hashbrowns / by Kim Bolton and Chris Wave.
      p.   cm.
   ISBN 0-07788-171-5 (pbk.)
    1. Christian women—Religious life.   2. Christian Life. I. Wave
Chris, 1957- . II. Title.
BV4527.B64   1999
242'.643—dc21
                                             99-37033
                                             CIP

05 04 03 02 01 00 99

10 9 8 7 6 5 4 3 2 1

Contents

Introduction

od is in the restaurant business. Specifically, he is in the *diner* business. And the diner is in your neighborhood. The local diner is where the whole of humanity crosses paths. Big, little, single, married, rich, poor—everyone enters a diner sometime. If you hail from France, you will probably call this place a *café*. If you hail from Brazil, you'll call it a *caffé*. From Italy, a *trattoria*. But whatever you call it, life for the human race happens here.

And if diners are the meeting places for humanity, then that is where you will find God. He is the diner's head cook. To most of us, this comes as news, but it is true. He is not just the overseer or the absent facility owner. He is the *cook*. He is the Master Cook.

He began cooking at Creation. He cooked up a world and then creatures to inhabit that world. He cooked up a bunch of human beings because he wanted company, community.

And now he is cooking to feed the soul of the community. God is usually a creator of simple fare. He uses daily trials and occurrences of life to grow us in profound ways. His menu is varied, the ingredients ever-changing. Feeding and building a strong soul is always the goal.

The Girlville Diner is God's diner. Nothing happens here without the Cook knowing about it. He hopes his patrons are pleased with the food. But mostly he is concerned with serving nourishing fare. He feeds the spirit. Sometimes the meat is tough or doesn't taste so good to us. But the community grows on this food—strong in the secret soul place.

1

Hash Browns and Other Comfort Food

Stories about Finding Contentment

In the world of food, as in the world of contentment, true comfort usually comes wrapped in a simple package, a package that belies the effort and time gone into its preparation.

We chase that elusive and simple package called contentment as if we were in a never-ending scavenger hunt. We pursue it by plying ourselves with instant comforts. "Maybe a new love will bring me contentment," we say. "Maybe when I lose ten pounds I'll feel content."

Contentment, like hash browns, looks like a simple thing. What is not seen at the dinner plate is the grating, shaping, and seasoning that has occurred behind the scenes, in the kitchen. Contentment is hard work. There is a measure of uncomfortable toil to be worked through before it can be learned.

Praying for simple things—to find a lost ring or to catch sight of a certain bird—seems, to the undiscerning soul, to square with God's desire for us. After all, what could it hurt to have that ring back now or glimpse an elusive bird? How simple the desire, how pure the request.

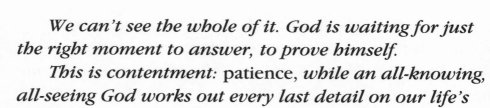

We can't see the whole of it. God is waiting for just the right moment to answer, to prove himself.

This is contentment: patience, *while an all-knowing, all-seeing God works out every last detail on our life's plate.*

A TOOTHBRUSH OF ONE'S OWN

There isn't much I require in this world. I don't need an entire room for myself. (My children would only pound on the door anyway.) I don't need fancy clothes or dancing shoes (I'm too tired even to take the garbage out at night. I could never muster up the energy to go dancing). A smattering of food every day and a dry toothbrush with no hair stuck in it is all I need. These are simple requests. Easily met, you may say.

Easily met unless you live with small children.

Not long ago I noticed I was no longer brushing my teeth with dry bristles. I wondered why. I noticed my husband now placed his toothbrush on a high shelf in the bathroom instead of the usual place, in the cabinet. *Strange,* I thought. Was he experiencing damp brush syndrome also?

I pondered the mystery of the damp bristles further. I realized something: A certain four-year-old girl had buried her Cinderella toothbrush bristle-side down in the dirt in the backyard. Yet it had not been missed for three weeks. *Curious,* I thought.

This four-year-old girl seemed a likely perpetrator. Since direct questioning of a suspect is too confrontational and rarely successful, I decided to set up a sting operation. I placed my brush on the high shelf next to my husband's brush.

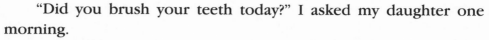

"Did you brush your teeth today?" I asked my daughter one morning.

"I can't find your toothbrush," she replied, not missing a beat.

The prewetted-bristle angst was only the beginning of my toothbrush agony. Something much worse was on the horizon for this mommy. While pregnant with my third child, the *hairy* brush syndrome started. By this point I had learned to tuck my toothbrush into the back of an empty drawer for protection from marauding toddlers. This happened to be the exact place the girls decided to dump their used hairy "bee-bops." These cloth-covered rubber bands were forcefully ripped from pig tails and braids each night and then tossed into my toothbrush drawer. So much hair was twisted up in these doo-hickeys, I was certain I would find a bleeding skull somewhere in the house.

Wads of hair married themselves to my toothbrush at the back of the drawer. The hairy couple then waited eagerly all night to trigger my hypersensitive gag reflex come morning. And gag I did.

I ranted and raved about needing *my space* during these difficult toddler years. I longed for something that was *my own.* "I need to have my own toothbrush! I need to be in the bathroom by myself *alone* for five minutes! I need . . . I need," I cried. This was the season of my discontent.

And then, one day it was over. My daughters grew out of toddlerhood. They learned to keep their toothbrushes in their own bathroom. All was calm on the toothbrush front.

Today, half a decade later, I open the drawer and I think, *some-*

thing is missing. I don't miss the hair in my bristles and I really like having a dry brush each day. But I dearly miss those little girls who so wanted to be like Mommy that they used anything within their reach belonging to me—my bathroom drawer, my toothbrush. They wanted to feel close to me. They wanted their things next to mine. I miss the little girls who so longed to be a part of my every waking minute that they placed their hairy bee-bops precisely next to my toothbrush.

Hindsight is a bittersweet thing. I wish I could go back and quietly pick the hairs out of my toothbrush without whining. And I would be content now to brush with the damp bristles of a shared toothbrush.

It was over so soon. My little girls are growing up. They are very busy now, busy with friends—and they don't notice me so much anymore. I miss them. I wish I had another chance. I would make those years last longer. I wouldn't wish the time away. Maybe I'll sneak into the girls' bathroom and stick my toothbrush next to theirs. I hope they notice. ■

—CW

THE RING

One spring, I realized I was missing a ring. It wasn't an expensive ring, but my husband, Tony, had given it to me when we first got married. It was a sentimental thing.

I called everyone I knew to see if I had left it anywhere. I called my mom. "Did I take that ring off while I was doing dishes at your house?"

"No," she said.

Nobody had seen that ring. "That ring is somewhere, Lord. Hey, Lord, what about that ring? I know you know where it is. Would you please get it to show up? When I find it, I'll be like the woman in the parable with the lost coin. I'm going to shout my find from the rooftops. I'm going to call all my friends and family. I've already called all of them to sweep out their houses. Now I'm just gonna wait."

Summer came and went, and I put all thoughts of the ring in the back of my mind. In September, Tony and I had a string of musical engagements in north Atlanta. We packed the family in the van—four kids, two car seats, two strollers, two diaper bags, two of everything. Videos, tapes, games, toys, and food, all packed in the van, and electronic equipment in the trailer behind it.

We sang Friday night, Saturday night, Sunday morning, and Sunday night. Every engagement was in a different place. To get the girls back home and into school Monday morning, we needed to leave Atlanta by nine. We knew the route and the routine. With the kids asleep in the car, we'd get home by three, sleep till six, and the kids could catch the school bus at seven. Perfect.

"Right on schedule," Tony said as we were toolin' along. And then he said, "Kim, do you hear that noise?"

"What noise?"

We've never broken down in all of our twenty years of traveling.

"I think we have a flat tire." He listened to the bumping sound carefully. "It's a flat on the trailer, and I don't have a spare for the trailer. There's a gas station. If it's a real gas station it won't take long at all."

We pulled off the exit and drove right to the station. It wasn't a real gas station; it was a food store with gas pumps. But I wasn't worried. Tony can fix anything. I figured he'd duct tape it if he had to.

But before Tony could even *think* about what to do, eight big guys surrounded the van and trailer. One man had a glazed-over look, sweating profusely on this chilly evening. The smell of alcohol surrounded the van. The men forcefully offered us their help. Several times. Tony thanked them each time and said he could handle it. Ignoring his refusals of assistance, they took the spare tire off of the van. Then they started taking the trailer tire off. Right before our eyes they began to strip our van and trailer.

One of them asked for money for helping with the tire change. Tony thought we'd better give him some. As Tony came up to the van window to get some cash, he said to me, "Kimberly, it's time to pray. Make sure all the doors are locked."

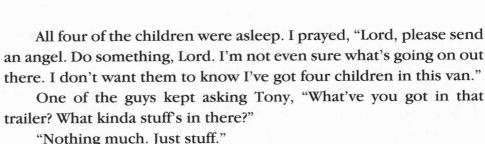

All four of the children were asleep. I prayed, "Lord, please send an angel. Do something, Lord. I'm not even sure what's going on out there. I don't want them to know I've got four children in this van."

One of the guys kept asking Tony, "What've you got in that trailer? What kinda stuff's in there?"

"Nothing much. Just stuff."

"Let's see if there's anything in the trailer to pull out and fix this thing." While one man distracted Tony, the others tried to get into the back of the trailer.

"Listen, I'm going to call a wrecker," said Tony. "I don't need any help. Thank you."

Right about that time (it was eleven o'clock), the gas station lights went off. They closed and locked up. The place went pitch dark. Everything was happening so fast. Eight guys surrounding Tony and the van.

The girls woke up. "What's the matter, Mom?"

"Well, nothing yet. Your dad's trying to fix a tire."

"Looks like he has a lot of help out there."

"I know it looks like it, but they're not really helping."

"Are we in trouble, Mom?"

At this point, we would have driven on the tire rim if we could have gotten out of there. But we couldn't. We were stuck. The wheel was already off the trailer, and the situation was rapidly getting worse. The man who seemed to be on drugs started talking faster and faster. Two others began arguing about who was there first and who should get the money.

"Amber, what was the Bible verse you learned this week?" I asked my daughter.

"'Put on the whole armor of God.'"

"Okay, let's put on our helmet, that breastplate, tie tight your shoes of peace. Here's another one: 'God didn't give us a spirit of fear, but power, love, and a sound mind.' Girls, we need to concentrate on what God can do for us. And right now we need him to step in and get us out of here." And then I prayed, "God, give us creative wisdom to know what to do."

Then, ding-dong, all at once I remembered the cell phone. Underneath all the baby gear was the new phone. Trying not to sound afraid or excited, I dialed the operator. "Hello, I'm at exit 11, the Dorcet exit on I-65. We are surrounded by eight guys we don't know. My husband is outside, and I'm inside our van with our four children. We are not in an emergency situation yet, but I would like for someone to come. Someone with authority. Someone in a uniform. Someone official, with a car that has a blue light. My children are in the vehicle. Do you have children? Do you understand what I'm trying to say?"

"Yes, I understand." There was a long pause. "But you're not at exit 11 on I-65. There is no Dorcet exit on I-65."

"I'm *telling* you I'm looking at the sign. I know this route. I'm coming from Atlanta to Fort Walton Beach and I'm at exit 11. Please, I have four children. Do you have children?"

"Yes, I have children, but you're not on I-65."

"Where am I?"

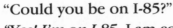

"Could you be on I-85?"

"Yes! I'm on I-85. I am coming from Atlanta headed south. I have not yet made it to Montgomery."

"I'll have someone right there. Let me transfer you to the Dorcet Police Department. I'll be thinking about you." Something about her kind manner comforted me. She transferred me straight in.

A voice answered slow and lazy, "Off..ic..er Graaanspaugh." Of course, I had to be talking to the one officer who seemed to have all the time in the world. I wanted to scream.

"Hello, sir," I said and went through the whole thing again: "I have four children in my van and we're surrounded by eight men. I'm not in trouble yet, but it looks like there's going to be trouble. Could you please send some authority? Soon?"

Another slow response. "Yeeees . . . Where . . . might . . . ya'll . . . beee?"

"Exit 11, I-85, at the gas station up on the hill."

Even more slowly, and drawling every word, he said, "IIII'll seeeeend . . . someooooooone . . . out diiiirectly."

"Tonight."

"Yeeees."

Ninety seconds later, a car pulled up, lights flashing, gravel spitting on the pavement, and Officer Barney Fife jumped out. He looked straight at Tony and said, "I don't need any trouble. I'm retiring in two weeks and do you know what kind of paperwork an incident like this requires?"

Tony replied, "These guys are all over my van. I can't get them out of here. I need some help."

The man who seemed to be on drugs said to the police officer, "I've got a gun."

"I've got a gun, too, Joe," Barney replied. Obviously he knew the man.

"No," Joe said. "I don't wan . . . I don't wan . . . you . . . give me any trouble." Back and forth the talk and guns went, all around my kids and my van, with my husband in the middle of it. The cop wooed the drug-crazed guy away, saying, "Come on over here, Joe. Come on, get over here."

As the officer pulled the guy away, Tony came to the van and said, "Kimberly, is there a coat in the van? It's really cold."

September is not usually cold in the South.

My daughter found a jacket underneath the back seat of the van. Tony slipped it on. Joe and Barney Fife were now having it out in front of us. The tension was thick. Tony came back to the van. He had a smile on his face. "Look what I found in the pocket of this jacket."

I looked. "Hey girls," I said, "you can go back to sleep. Jesus just showed up."

It was my gold ring.

If God cared so much about my gold ring that cost nearly nothing and was just sentimental to me, how much more does he care about the things that are most precious?

We got a wrecker that took us all the way into the Union 76 gas

station in Montgomery. Fixed our tire and got us home. We pulled into our driveway just in time to get the kids off to school.

Is God good or what? All the way home I thanked God for all that he meant to me, all that he provided for us. I needed the miracle of the ring six months after I lost it, and God knew that. His timing is perfect.■

—KB

THE NAKED MAN

Tony (my husband) and I worked out a nocturnal tag-team operation with all four of our children. I took the first shift (10:00 P.M. to 3:00 A.M.). He took the second shift (3:00 A.M. to 7:00 A.M.). This arrangement gave me hope. Thinking I might sleep four hours straight saved me from despair.

On this particular night, I was snuggled in between my sheets. It was ten minutes before ten o'clock. I was praying and praying because I remembered what my mother always taught me: "If you can't fall asleep, you need to pray. The devil doesn't want you to pray so he'll leave you alone and let you go to sleep." I know this isn't Scripture, but it works for me.

"Lord, please let me sleep. Let all of these children sleep on my shift. If they have to wake up, let it be on Tony's shift."

The baby woke on my shift. I staggered off in the direction of the wailing baby. I rocked and swayed with the baby. I sang, patted, and prayed for ninety minutes. Ninety long minutes.

I sang:

Jesus loves me this I know.

You should be asleep, you know. . . .

Go to sleep, Baby.

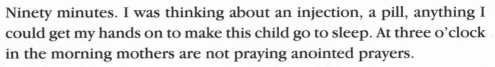

Ninety minutes. I was thinking about an injection, a pill, anything I could get my hands on to make this child go to sleep. At three o'clock in the morning mothers are not praying anointed prayers.

Jesus loves me this I know.

Go to sleep, Baby, and we'll all know . . .

I wanted my bed and nothing more. I would not be able to handle tomorrow if I did not get into bed soon.

Three-thirty A.M. I crawled back to bed, wasted.

Please, no, it can't be. I heard the other one coming down the hall. I threw back the covers and patted the bed. "Come on, just get in bed with me," I said without turning to look at her.

She wouldn't budge. I could hear her breathing, but she wouldn't move. I thought, *Okay kid, go ahead and sleep on the floor, but you're gonna freeze.*

A few minutes later, I said it again, "Come on, get in bed with me. It's cold."

No movement. Only breathing.

Finally, that mother gene kicked in, and I thought she needed to be off the cold floor. I said, "Please get in bed with me, now." I turned over to look at her only to discover that this was not my child. It was a man. A naked man.

He was down on all fours, naked, and covered with whipped cream. He was so close, I could almost touch him.

I pinched my own left hand with my right to make sure I was really awake and not dreaming. I was awake.

"What in the world are you doing here?" I asked out loud.

I reached behind me to shake Tony into consciousness, calling him in a screaming whisper as I kept my eyes on the naked man, "Tony . . . Tony . . . Tony!" I shook him hard. He turned a sleepy eye in my direction and said, "What's your sister doing here?" (The only thing my sister had in common with this man is that they're both blond.)

"That's not my sister," I whispered.

"Who is it?"

"I don't know."

"What is it?"

"It's a naked man in our room!" We were chit-chatting about this froth-covered man who was listening to every word we said, still down on all fours. His behind was in the air and his head was on the floor. Tony and I were discussing his presence after I'd asked him to get in bed with me—three times!

Suddenly, the naked man freaked. He grabbed the phone and zinged it at Tony's head. Blood started gushing in every direction. And the man ran off.

We checked under beds and in closets to see if he was working in tandem. Was there another whipped cream–covered man somewhere in my house? Satisfied that he came alone, we called the police. The naked man was long gone.

The police finished their report, and I was left with a different house. This was now a house someone evil had entered uninvited, leaving fear in his wake. This somebody knew how I slept. He knew

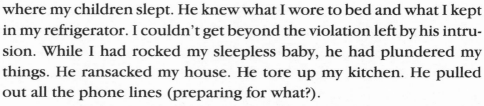

where my children slept. He knew what I wore to bed and what I kept in my refrigerator. I couldn't get beyond the violation left by his intrusion. While I had rocked my sleepless baby, he had plundered my things. He ransacked my house. He tore up my kitchen. He pulled out all the phone lines (preparing for what?).

I was unable to sleep through the night anymore. I started doing laundry at all kinds of crazy hours. Two weeks later, I was shaking out a sheet from the dryer at two o'clock in the morning. I looked up and saw the front door handle turn. This time I yelled. Tony came running. The guy ran off, but the locks had been chiseled off the front door.

Somebody's after me. Somebody's after my kids. What's he going to do to us when he gets us? Why does he want me? All the locks in the world won't keep him out. What am I going to do? I can't get away. These thoughts continually ran through my head.

Drowning in fear, I stopped sleeping altogether. I became bitter and judgmental. I blamed Tony for not protecting me. I said to him in anger, "If you're such a great husband, why didn't you get that guy and kill him? Why didn't you run after him?"

No one hurt as I did. No one knew how I was feeling. Fear strangled all my reason and perspective. I was caught in its jaws and couldn't get loose. It was ransacking my life.

Six weeks into this nightmare, Tony came to me, put his hands on my shoulders and said, "You're going crazy, and you're driving the rest of us crazy too. You'd better get a hold of God."

I turned away from him; I was in pain. But later, alone in my room, I realized he was right. I cried out to God. I turned to the back of my Bible. I looked under the index listings for *fear*, *peace*, and *sleep*, because those words were huge in my mind. I was terribly afraid. I didn't have an ounce of peace and I hadn't slept in six weeks. I wrote down on a 5 x 7 sheet of paper every verse listed under those headings.

"What time I am afraid, I will trust in Thee." "Fear not, for I am with thee." "I will keep in perfect peace those whose minds are stayed on Me." "When you go through the fire, you will not be burned and when you go through the waters you will not drown." "I will lie down and sleep in peace." "Your sleep will be sweet and you will dwell in safety." "He will give his angels charge over you." "I will never leave you or forsake you." "I will not relax my hold on you." "I will not fail you." "You can boldly and with confidence say, 'the Lord is my helper.'"

I didn't believe a word of it. But I wrote all those verses down. I kept that slip of paper in my pocket by day. I lay down every night with those verses on my chest. I asked God to permeate my being with those verses. I said those verses out loud, believing that faith would come by hearing, and hearing by the Word of God. My mouth said them and my spirit heard them.

Slowly, over a stretch of time, my faith increased. God was healing me. Three months after those incidents, I woke up with a new interpretation of the event. The facts remained the same. What had changed was how I saw those facts.

A naked man broke into my house, I thought. *He was so close I*

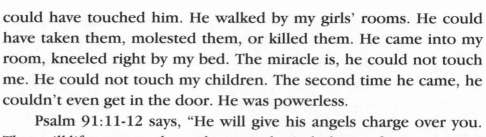

could have touched him. He walked by my girls' rooms. He could have taken them, molested them, or killed them. He came into my room, kneeled right by my bed. The miracle is, he could not touch me. He could not touch my children. The second time he came, he couldn't even get in the door. He was powerless.

Psalm 91:11-12 says, "He will give his angels charge over you. They will lift you over the rock so you don't dash your foot against it." I had a boulder in my life. A boulder of fear and doubt. The angels of God lifted me over it.■

—KB

KIWI IN MOUSE CLOTHING

My almost-blind Granny was best known for her plain, Midwestern cooking. Her culinary skills were honed during the war using items from the ration list. Grandma never used food with funny names like "ugli fruit" or ate daring crosses like apple-pear. She lived in a tiny, Midwestern town that considered bananas exotic.

One day my father, desiring to expand his mother's horizons, purchased a kiwi fruit for Grandma. Gram had never seen or heard of kiwi. In a hurry to get home to his family, Dad failed to tell her about the additional fruit as he placed the sack of groceries on Gram's kitchen table.

Grandma unpacked her plain cheese, her plain milk, her plain coffee. Then she unpacked . . . *oh my, what is that small, hard, furry thing?—Eek! A mouse!*

The "mouse" rolled out of the bag. Grandma snatched her trusty broom from the corner. She chased the mouse around the kitchen and battered it until it was reduced to a pulpy mess. A mess she took to be mouse guts.

I batter phantom guts around too. I see God's gifts to me, but sometimes they don't look like gifts, they look like vermin. Seeing through my narrow field of sight, that tunnel vision of my own

31

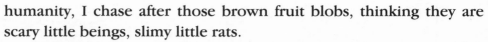

humanity, I chase after those brown fruit blobs, thinking they are scary little beings, slimy little rats.

I beat and beat those "mice" around with my broom of misunderstanding, my broom of fear and discontent. I say to God, "Why this? Why this hideous little thing scampering across my floor?" Sometimes I ask God to take the little mouse and go away—leave me be.

But when the mouse (and God) show no sign of taking their leave—when I have exhausted my bag of annoyed and angry appeals—when I have beat the thing in front of me to a pulpy mess and still don't know anything, then I do the only thing left. I settle my fretful spirit. I quiet down. I try to figure out what this mouse actually is, what I'm supposed to learn.

In those chases I've decided I know exactly what God is up to. I believe, somehow, I can read his holy mind. "Oh yes, God," I say. "You must be doing thus and such, and I am supposed to do such and thus. And once I do that such and thus, then this icky mousy thing happening to me will be over."

Ha!

Read the mind of the God who delights in confounding the worldly wise with foolish things? Read the mind of the God who makes the first, last, and the last, first? That's like trying to decode The Holiest Mind with a plastic Dick Tracy decoder watch. This is *God*—tricky God—who sends blessing-kiwis that for all the world look more like mouse-curses.

Who can read his holy mind? Who can understand his kiwi gifts?

The gift I most often fail to recognize (or *want* to recognize) is *the gift of pain.* Years ago I listened to the final gasps of a diseased, and dying relationship. I felt God was leaving me alone in a "mouse"-infested place. "Where are you?" I asked at least a billion times. I could not imagine any good thing coming of this very deep and visceral pain. I could not imagine ever being a whole person after chasing this painful mouse around to my exhaustion.

Pain is not something a sane person wishes for. It is gut-wrenching and soul-draining. But this pain, for me, was a kiwi in mouse clothing. I grew a little stronger, and a bit wiser because of it.

Like it or not, I learn best when I hurt. When I stop shouting at God about my discomfort—when I tape my mouth closed and listen, I realize that pain can be a gift, a kiwi.

God is a patient god. Despite my desperate pleas for an easy life and my blindness to the good in doing things his way, God continues to hang in there with me. He listens to me whine at each difficult pass in my road. And he heaps bags of blessings on my table, kiwis by the truckload. I think he hopes that one day I won't automatically look at the good gift he's placed before me and think . . . *oh my, what is that thing?* and then scream, "Mouse!" as I run for the broom.■

—CW

CAMPERS ON THE RIDGE

L ast summer opened up with several long, droughty weeks. Two dog-hot summer months passed without a single drop from the skies.

"Let's go camping!" my husband said. Camping for us is like a rain dance to the Native American. It always works. The Midwest was suffering in the burn out and heat, and I thought it our civic duty to do all we could for the rain effort.

The van was stuffed full of camping gear as we headed for a week in the North Woods. The kids had to squish between bicycles, coolers, firewood, and the camp stove. To cushion their bones from bicycle handles, they used loaves of bread.

We set up housekeeping in a perfect, open-to-wind-and-weather crescent-shaped site at the tip of the highest butte my husband could find. The site was in the stratosphere. Typical of most airline pilots, my husband is happiest at nose bleed heights. He requires 40,000 feet of air space beneath him to breathe properly.

An hour into setup on the heights, I felt the first few raindrops. Civic duty camping was paying off. My husband—a man of three passions: eating, meteorology, and sleeping (in that order)—interrupted his usually lengthy repast to triple-secure our tent and carefully watch the sky.

34

Alarms should have sounded when he did not immediately return to his roasted corn because he was bungee-ing the tent to a 400-year-old oak tree. A prudent wife would have panicked as he continued to putter about the site letting dinner grow cold.

Instead, I chalked his unusual behavior up to excitement over our wilderness excursion. After dinner, I zipped the children into their bags, and they dropped off to sleep inside the tent.

"Getting a little stormy," I said to the putterer.

"Just an isolated cell," he assured me in a pilot-kind-of-way. And he began mumbling unintelligibly as he dickered around the tent. He was busy threading ropes and anchor lines from tree to tree like a giant nest of interwoven spider webs.

Though I found myself getting caught in the spaghetti of bungee cords and nylon rope he was using to anchor our tent, I felt confident as I noted we appeared well-secured to the minivan as well as to the country of China.

It appeared that I was not the only one wondering at the strange weavings. Our camping neighbors began to stare at the intricate web of anchor lines that my husband, Charlotte the spider, had spun in our campsite. As yet, I was unalarmed. *He's a putterer,* I reminded myself.

The raindrops grew fat as we climbed inside the tent. Soon they began to thump against the tent like large, dropping tropical fruits. *Like pineapples,* I thought.

"Just an isolated cell," he said again as he turned over in his sleeping bag.

My husband is known to be unflappable in the most frightening of circumstances.

Quietly over in his corner of the tent he slept as the wind picked up to gale force. I tried to sleep. I herded the kids into the center of the tent and crawled in closer to my husband.

Bulging gusts of wind mixed with hail began to pound all sides of the tent. Rain flaps blew in from both sides, kissing in the middle as the wind whipped wildly from every direction. Lightning snapped and cracked so near to us that I felt the hair on my arms stand at attention.

This is really great that we are up here on Mt. Kilimanjaro like human lightning rods, I thought. *I've got a good idea, why don't we wrap ourselves in tin foil?* My husband didn't move. A sound like a speeding train roared around our campsite. With the storm noises screaming in our ears, I couldn't communicate with my children. And no one could communicate with the sleeping spider.

I do not become milk-livered in a storm. I *like* storms. But this was beyond "storm." This was a dry-land typhoon, and my babies and I were in a tent.

I tried not to worry, reciting Bible verses to myself: "Peace be still . . ." I began. I moved to "Fear not, for I am with you. . . . " Then I said, "Help, God. Give me faith. This is very scary. Send help, send an angel." By now the children were crying. "O.K., let's make a run for the car," was my suggestion.

"Too dangerous," said the calm pilot voice between crashes of thunder.

"'Too dangerous?' How can you say 'too dangerous,' calmly? Too dangerous to run for the shelter of two tons of steel? If you want to talk about dangerous, let's talk about *nylon tent!"*

I was thinking, *Why isn't that park ranger coming to evacuate us?* But I knew why. Rangers don't check up on campers when it's not even safe to travel in a heavy-duty all-terrain vehicle.

Lightning crashed forcefully and with jarring frequency up there on Kilimanjaro. It felt too treacherous to uncurl from our family huddle. The sides of the tent collapsed in on the floor. They popped back out again. The web of cords popped. The ties pulled free of the tent stakes. Now we were strung by two cords—the one to the van and the one tied to the ancient oak with roots in China.

My husband seemed only mildly concerned. *He knows more about weather than I do. We must be O.K. No need to flip out if he isn't panicky.*

The blackness inside the tent was broken by streaks of lightning. I looked over where I thought my husband was cuddling a screaming child. Instead I saw him folded over on his knees.

Now, I know my husband to be a praying man. I have seen him on his knees many times, seeking God. But I have never seen him folded so low over his knees. He was fetal, almost in a ball. The king of composure cracked! *He's out of his mind with fear and not telling me!* This posture for my husband was sheer, unadulterated alarm.

"Squalls like this don't last long," he said. Only they did last long. Two hours long. (In tent hours that's *ten.*)

No angel ever showed up at the door of my tent even though I

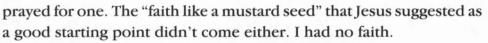

prayed for one. The "faith like a mustard seed" that Jesus suggested as a good starting point didn't come either. I had no faith.

When a bad thing happens I always look for the M&M (moral in the misery). *What was that all about, Lord? Why didn't you send somebody to help us? Was letting us go through a ten-on-the-Richter-scale storm necessary? A seven would have sufficed to rattle my cage sufficiently.* But as far as I could see there was no M&M.

The next morning, as we exited the saturated, drippy tent, we looked around us at what appeared to be exploded land mines, the remains of campsites. Most of the campers had packed up in the storm and moved out.

"Wimps," I said. The couple in the orange tent next door, the ones who spent more time staring at my web-spinning Charlotte than they did securing their own tent, looked like two dead logs under a limp piece of lettuce. Their tent collapsed on top of them after it pulled free from the ground. Bungee cords and rope pieces lay all around their site like beaten, dead snakes.

I looked around with pride at my Spider man after seeing we were the only upright tent in the area.

The ranger pulled up just then.

"Ya hey!" he said, all jovial-like. "Mighty bad storm last night."

"I'm kind of surprised you didn't evacuate us. Weren't you worried about us up here?" I asked, sort of accusingly.

"Oh, we were watching—riding around checking everybody on the ridge—not the first time for a bad storm. You get to know these storms. We know the evac point," he said as he rolled away.

So they were watching out for us. God and that ranger, who was riding around in the car—watching our camp gear blow around like confetti.

Well . . . anyway, *God* was there. It seems he told the Kilimanjaro storm it could drop tropical fruit raindrops for two hours only. No longer than that. He told the wind it could whip up fifty of the fifty-two stakes securing our tent. But it could not touch the last two. God, it seems, said to the lightning, "You can strike this close, but no closer."

Yes, I believe God was out there checking on us. I'm just not convinced mister *ya-hey,* the ranger, was riding around up there that night in the middle of the storm at the top of the ridge.■

—CW

SLAYING THOSE DRAGONS

The first I think I knew that life was *not* a fairy tale was when my husband Tony and I sang at a youth group retreat camp in north Georgia.

Dinner at the camp that first night consisted of a formless, spaghetti-mush type thing. Awful, horrible stuff. We sat down to eat the concoction. My older daughters sat at one table. I chose a seat at the head of an eight-foot long, picnic-style table, because it had a lot of room. My sixteen-month-old baby needed all the baby paraphernalia space I could get him.

Then a bell clanged. The campers sprang into well-rehearsed action. They knew this dinner routine. I *didn't*.

In a matter of seconds dirty plates with partially consumed spaghetti mush started coming my way. The campers cleaned and scraped off the mush remains into one huge bowl—a bowl right by me and my baby.

Sixteen iced-tea glasses, sixteen plates were passed down hand to hand until they all piled up to my nose where I sat next to my clean baby. The rule of the camp stated: The one on the end busses the table and hauls the dishes into the kitchen. That was me, the one on the end, the guest of honor. The mother with the baby. Dishes, garbage, food . . . everywhere. Noise, kids, mush, bugs . . . everywhere.

I was frustrated and tired and scheduled to sing at eleven. *P.M.*

Youth camps don't schedule anything at a normal hour. They do things late, especially on a Saturday night. Tony and I sing for church groups and conferences and we had already sung somewhere else Thursday and Friday nights. Now, here I was on this Saturday night, worn out, spent, used up.

"Bring linens from home," the camp leaders told me when we were making arrangements. I guess that should have been the first clue. After I bussed the tables, I searched for my room in the "staff quarters."

A shower, yes, a shower will make me feel better. The shower curtain hung from two hooks at each end, leaving a baggy droop in the middle. It wasn't really even a shower. It was a cinder-block cubby hole with a pipe coming out of the wall. The floor must have had colored tile covering it at one time, but now that color was not imaginable. My feet stuck to bland, colorless pieces of shower floor beneath me.

Having showered, I surveyed my living quarters. My bed was a pallet of some sort. Two pieces of foam rubber stuck together with duct tape. The windows had no screens and, of course, no air circulated. Bugs swooped and swarmed everywhere. To make up my bed I had brought thin, seven-year-old Sesame Street sheets belonging to my girls. But I didn't make up the bed. The stifling heat and swooping bugs drove me back to the van. *It will be better in there. It will be cool in there,* I thought. I took my baby boy and went out to the parking lot.

But it wasn't better in the van. It was worse. Hot, cramped, and lonely. This whole thing was bigger than me. It was a big dragon.

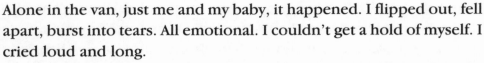

Alone in the van, just me and my baby, it happened. I flipped out, fell apart, burst into tears. All emotional. I couldn't get a hold of myself. I cried loud and long.

I turned on the radio. A pastor was serving communion in California. He said, "Take your bread. . . ." I took my imaginary bread and repeated after him, "I take my bread. . . . Lord, I thank you for your sacrifice."

I broke up again. I blubbered and slobbered all over the place. I gave my baby a little piece of imaginary bread and said through my fits of sobbing, "Here, Baby, eat this." I was not a bit thankful. I was sad. Really sad. I was tired. I hated doing this to my kids. I hated this crazy road life that we'd been living for nearly twenty years.

Tony came around looking for us. When he saw the mess I was, he whispered, "Kimberly, what's wrong with you?"

I stammered, "I ha—I ha—I hate it here. It's dir—dir—dirty."

He took me back to our room to show me what might be good about it. But even Tony couldn't find anything good. There was nothing good about that room.

He made the bed with the Sesame Street sheets and tried to console me. He said, "I'll do the ministry tonight by myself. You stay here."

Never before had I missed a performance. Tony had no idea how that touched me. His supernatural gentleness that night gave me the break I needed—at that moment I most needed it.

After getting back home from the camp, I lunched with a friend. I told her about the horrendous weekend, my psychotic episode, and the dragon I felt breathing down my neck. "There is no way God called me to be a minister before he called me to be a mother," I said.

She placed her hand on mine and said, "No, he didn't; he called you to be a wife before he called you to be any of those." I was pierced. This road ministry was something Tony believed we should be doing.

After lunch that day, I read something that changed my perspective—something new to me. I couldn't believe it was in the Bible. It was big. There in the book of Ephesians I read: "Let all bitterness and indignation, wrath and passion, rage and bad temper, resentment, anger and animosity, quarreling, brawling, clamor, contention, slander and evil speaking, abusive or blasphemous language, be banished from you. All malice, spite, ill will, or baseness of any kind." God, I began to realize, often calls me into difficult situations. But God told me *how to be* in those difficulties.

I took a deep breath. There was more. "Become useful, helpful, kind to one another, tenderhearted, compassionate, understanding, loving-hearted, forgiving one another readily and freely as God in Christ forgave you."

Who can do all that? I thought. *I can't do that. I don't want to do that.* The trouble was that the Bible wasn't saying, "if you feel like it" or "if you can," it was saying *do it.*

Then I flipped back a few pages to Corinthians and read a short little sentence: "I am not my own." The words dug deep into me. *Clearly,* I realized, *I am created to give glory to God, not to my own self or my own self-will.*

Those three Bible passages applied to every dragon I must fight in my life. Those verses aren't easy, but they are true.

There and then I changed my attitude. I determined to become thankful for the challenges. I determined to respect my husband's decision to do ministry on the road.

Now I no longer focus on how difficult the road might be. This is not a fairy tale life, I've discovered. But those verses of Scripture are sharp swords. And with those swords I am able to defeat those dragons of difficult circumstance.■

—KB

POULTRYGEIST

B e careful what you pray for." Everybody says it. Who would think that kind of warning would apply to prayers about birds? Specifically, *bluebirds* and your teensy little, "Lord, just let me see one, please"?

Last spring, I thought it good and right for my children to behold a true prairie native: the Eastern bluebird. I chose to hunt for this bluebird for two reasons. One, people with knowledge about extinction issues were spending untold time and treasure coaxing that little bird back from the brink of the lost. It added just enough spicy challenge to my hunt to know that it was thrillingly possible to see this rare-but-not-too-elusive bird.

The second, more important reason I sought a glimpse of this bird was because I bore the distinction of being a "Bluebird" when I was in grade school. *Bluebird* was the junior division of Camp Fire Girls. And though being a Brownie was the universally cool thing to do at the time, the girls in my neighborhood were doing the Bluebird gig.

I came to love my Bluebird affiliation because we had very hip uniforms: cute red vests with blue beanie caps. Today, thirty-four years hence, I have a soft place for bluebirds of any kind.

Our attempts to snag a glimpse of that Eastern bluebird began in earnest. To attract bluebirds, it is necessary to have a prairie, so we

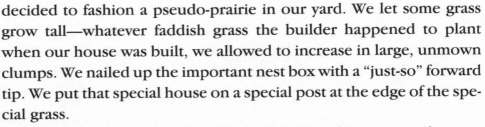

decided to fashion a pseudo-prairie in our yard. We let some grass grow tall—whatever faddish grass the builder happened to plant when our house was built, we allowed to increase in large, unmown clumps. We nailed up the important nest box with a "just-so" forward tip. We put that special house on a special post at the edge of the special grass.

We waited. We waited and waited. For weeks, we waited.

Because children are easily distracted by lengthy waiting periods, I thought, *Since God thought to make the birds and knows the mind of a bluebird, I will ask him to send us one soon.* So I prayed to see a bluebird.

And then, around the first of May, a blue-feathered couple arrived. They perched on the swing set, one at each end. He swooped and hollered around the bird house. He pecked at the corners, checked the security system, and made sure no disgusting sparrows occupied his dream home. Finally, he felt secure enough to let the Mrs. move in.

In my unbridled excitement at my first look, I left a long-distance friend dangling from the phone cord as I ran to retrieve my binoculars—and that would be the *last* time I would need binoculars to see this bird.

The next day, Mr. Eastern Bluebird mounted an assault on my house. Eight brand new, overpriced French doors and windows across the back of the house became his personal Goliath. He hated them. He let us know he hated them by leaving white protests everywhere.

"Oh well," we said. "Anything for a bluebird," as we cheerfully cleaned up the mess.

Every day thereafter, four hundred times a day, Mr. Bluebird flung his white calling-card challenges on the glass. We spritzed them away with blue window spray. With each day we grew less cheerful, knowing more angry sorties were to come.

A month later we began to murmur ungracious words in his presence like, "Have-a-Heart Trap." We didn't have a heart when we said this.

"Your husband is driving me nuts!" I screamed to Mrs. Bird-wife. She ignored me. I called Darlene. She knows everything a person can know about birds.

"Meal worms," she said. "Try meal worms. Maybe the worms will make him forget about you. Anyway, the mating season is almost over. He'll fly off soon." She didn't tell me what she meant by "soon," and I was afraid to ask.

I don't own a gun, but I began thinking about a gun.

Mr. Bluebird-husband thought we weren't paying enough attention to him, so he started peckering on the window in our bedroom at 5:25 A.M.—every A.M.—on the dot.

"Peck, peck, peck. Wake up and fight," he'd say. We tried shooing him away. He scooted off to a pine branch a few wing flips away, only to return with renewed vengeance and the white calling card.

I have endured this bird as long as humanly possible, I thought.

I rang up Darlene again.

"This bird is making me insane," I said. She told me a terrible

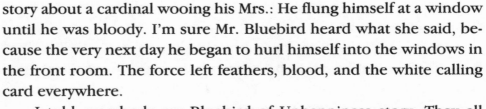

story about a cardinal wooing his Mrs.: He flung himself at a window until he was bloody. I'm sure Mr. Bluebird heard what she said, because the very next day he began to hurl himself into the windows in the front room. The force left feathers, blood, and the white calling card everywhere.

I told everybody my Bluebird of Unhappiness story. They all said, "Oh yes, I saw that once." And then they would tell me a story not even half as bad as mine. I would shake my head and say, "You don't know how bad my story is."

This Mr. Alfred Hitchcock-wannabe did not care a bit if I was out talking bad about him to the neighbors. He pooped and pecked with Lothario abandon.

Near the end of June, after we put plastic owls up, taped newspaper to the glass, and dangled various paraphernalia in the windows, the bird noticed the new brass handles we put on the overpriced French doors. He took to perching on them before he jettisoned into the glass—of course leaving his white calling card all over them, which eventually ate away at the finish.

A professional glass man came out to scrub bird impressions from the windows and brass door handles. Perfect outlines of birds with splayed wings painted the glass in every room.

I started to pray Mr. Bluebird would die.

Finally, one morning, he was gone. No *peck, peck, pecking* on the window. There was silence for the first time in months. We slept in until six o'clock.

I glanced back in my mind to my original, innocent request: "Please send a bluebird," I had said then.

Gee, God, what was that all about? What were you thinking? We just wanted to see a little birdie. We didn't need the Freddie Kruger of Bluebirdville.

God never did tell me what he was thinking. I'm pretty sure it has something to do with my not having the big picture, the bird's-eye view, like he has. All I want to say with this little story is, be careful—be very careful—what you pray for. ■

—CW

2
Grits, Crab Cakes, and Pot Luck

Stories about Soul Growth

We all have spates of pre-planned, organized soul growth. We map our recipe for the year's growth in the way that seems good to us human beings. Our recipe includes a portion of inspirational reading alone in a wooded area, a pinch of service to mankind in a faraway land, a serving of that week-long visit to the Trappist monastery. And voilà! The perfect ingredients for soul growth.

"Ha!" says God. As often is the case, God has a different recipe for growing a soul. The ingredients are not terribly exotic. They are common and available to anyone. The only requirement is: Show up at the table and don't skulk away when the going gets tough.

When God's potluck of growth is served, the temptation is to slip into our cozy, neurotic glove of denial. We want to eat somewhere else where the food is not so unpredictable. We want it nice, always. Nice *is* not a bad thing, but very little growth happens when things are nice. Nice is dessert. Dessert makes you fat. The gritty life, if observed while dining with God, shores up the spirit. Crab cakes, the difficult dinner that is the result of a lot of leftover, picked-over shells, is always worth the mess of preparation.

Soul growth at the diner is simple really. Eat your peas and carrots—not too much sugar. Do your hard work. Show up—dinner is served.

KENDRA

A dark cloud of bad news rolled in one Wednesday morning. And it hovered over my community for weeks. It came when I returned home following a morning of errands and absently listened to messages left on the answering machine.

I snapped to attention when I heard the following message from a friend:

> . . . pray for Kendra. . . . thought she had the flu . . . her heart is failing. . . .

No! This is not true! I thought. *Things like this don't happen to healthy, eleven-year-old girls.*

I then called my friends—Kendra's parents—anxious to hear their young daughter was fine, certain we would laugh together over the wild tales spawned by telephone chains.

"Tell me it isn't true," I begged Kendra's dad. He started to cry. His sadness covered my spirit with a thick, lead blanket.

I hung up the phone. I wish I could say I prayed right there and then. I *didn't*—I cried. I cried long and hard. I cried for my friends and the little girl I didn't have time to get to know. I cried for Kendra's sisters and her grandparents. I cried for the uncertainty of my own children's future. I cried until I was dry inside. Finally, the next morning, I prayed.

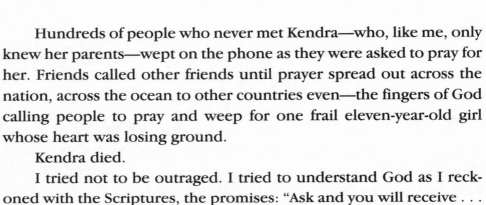

Hundreds of people who never met Kendra—who, like me, only knew her parents—wept on the phone as they were asked to pray for her. Friends called other friends until prayer spread out across the nation, across the ocean to other countries even—the fingers of God calling people to pray and weep for one frail eleven-year-old girl whose heart was losing ground.

Kendra died.

I tried not to be outraged. I tried to understand God as I reckoned with the Scriptures, the promises: "Ask and you will receive . . . Where two or more agree . . . it will be done." I *did* ask and thousands agreed. Still she died.

I couldn't go to the funeral that a trillion people turned out for. I did not know God anymore. I was on new, unsteady spiritual ground.

The world of faith and prayer took a downward turn for me. God became a big, black overcoat that I was forced to wear in this, the winter of my faith. The coat was cumbersome and far too shifty—but without him, without that coat, I was cold.

Why, why, why? I couldn't get beyond the grief, the anger. I didn't trust God anymore. I didn't know where to go with my rage. God was the last stop on this train—if his station was closed, where was I to get off?

I numbly and without feeling continued to ride around and around in a dizzying circle of hopelessness and anger. I prayed that when this runaway train of confusion came to a halt, I would know something about Kendra's death or my faith.

That didn't happen. It's been three years now, and the only thing

I have learned is that this is a world where easy answers are not to be had. Children get sick, and sometimes they die. Perhaps it is here in this lonely place of numbing anguish where God displays his most unwelcome power: The power to be sovereign. The power not to give all the answers.

I am always trying to give my grief wings by answering it—by filling in the gaps with reasons—hoping then that the grief will fly away. *Maybe,* I say to myself, *it is for* this *reason she died. . . . Maybe she died for* that *reason. . . .*

But the answers don't satisfy. And God, it seems, is silent.

I saw Kendra's mother recently. I wondered what was to be learned from her daughter's death. I couldn't think of anything. *Maybe,* I think, *it's not about learning something.* Maybe it's not about us at all. Maybe it is simply reading a manuscript of words in another language. A great work can be translated from French to English or Latin to Greek, but it's not the same with the language of heaven. It does not translate into the verbiage of earth. Maybe it will make sense when I am given the completed script, all of the words, in the right language. Maybe I will understand it on the other side of this world.■

—CW

IMMIGRANTS

Living on God's Land

Sometimes the things I know seem like pure piffle. I know a little bit of German, a useful phrase or two in case I ever become a nurse in Mexico, and enough French to eat well. Mostly, these language skills have served only to create verbal chaos in the countries I visit as a flight attendant.

In my travels I have noticed there is verbal chaos everywhere. Sometimes we are divided by linguistics, sometimes our barriers are geographic. More often, it seems, we, the inhabitants of this world, just don't seem to understand each other's differences.

One blizzardy night I received a call to crew a delayed airplane to Munich, Germany. As I boarded the plane, signs of unrest greeted me. Litter filled the aisle. Newspapers and magazines in two languages carpeted the area from the cockpit door back to the rear galley area. Egress with my "wheely" carry-on and big-girl shoes was nearly impossible. My suitcase fishtailed and slithered along the newspaper trail, and my spiky heels speared the trash.

Two hundred and thirty-two passengers had just spent the last six hours of their lives waiting for takeoff. Like obedient soldiers sitting upright and locked into their seats, these travelers rolled around on runways at the airport as the plane pulled in and out of takeoff lines for repeated de-icing. Finally the original crew exceeded their duty time and needed to be replaced.

Small personality flares erupted and spread all over the plane like prairie grass fires. The nerves of the frazzled crowd fermented to a moil. Tempers crescendoed, sucking the few remaining molecules of oxygen from the recirculated air. No one was happy. But 24E and 25E were particularly distraught.

He was a long, lanky fellow with long, even lankier legs folded double under the seat in front of him. Her seat. She was trying to enjoy the blackened airplane dinner that was not supposed to be blackened.

The tense pair began to argue vehemently in German, he leaning forward to shake her seat while she ate, she laying back her seat flat so that her hair rested in his dinner tray. He shoved his knees into her seat back; she flew forward into her mashed potatoes. The rest of the passengers, mostly German, stiffened in the tense air and looked to me, the poor working stiff in the aisle, to stomp out the flames between 24E and 25E.

I knew only two things to say in German: "I can't find my galoshes" and "Go straight ahead to the first stop light and turn left."

"Ich kann meine Gummischuhe nicht finden!" I said with the presence of a great orator—"I can't find my rubber shoes." Nobody laughed openly, but white paper napkins came up to mouths and a cacophony of nervous, pretend-coughs could be heard. My gift of verbal chaos de-stressed the moment, releasing some of the tension building inside the plane.

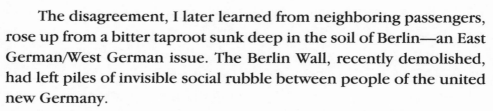

The disagreement, I later learned from neighboring passengers, rose up from a bitter taproot sunk deep in the soil of Berlin—an East German/West German issue. The Berlin Wall, recently demolished, had left piles of invisible social rubble between people of the united new Germany.

Social rubble is *everywhere,* not just in Germany. I feel sorry for God. He thought it would be nice for us to have different things to look at on Earth. He probably thought, *Hey, Heaven is stuffed with My amazing live art. I can't give them that yet but I'll give them a taste of the vibrant colors, shapes, styles, and sounds of this diverse place I live in. I'll slant their eyes and paint their skin. I'll make them male and female, give them small teeth, big teeth, straight hair, fuzzy hair. I'll make them sound different from each other. Won't they love discovering all the nifty, creative people I've designed?* I feel sorry for God. I think he's crying about this.

I think he's crying about our social rubble, about the irony of our making the gift of differences into battles.

Yesterday I read in the newspaper that my sleepy, untouched community hosted a murder. The beloved grocery store owner wasn't killed for money. We in the community almost could have understood that. It was a racist thing. An East/West thing. Ijama was Japanese. It's ironic that Ijama's murderer was Italian. He had black hair and straight eyes. He was trying to purge America of dirty foreigners.

Walls can be built and then torn down again, but the truth is we can't purge ethnicity from any land. We are all ethnic. We all have eyes that slant one way or the other. We all have strange accents. We are all immigrants living in temporary housing on God's land. And he is crying. God, the landlord, is crying.■

—CW

THE QUEEN BUSY BEE

My latest catalog order arrived last month. Bees. Ten thousand fuzzy, buzzy critters zipped and dipped through my hair and into my ears.

Bees are a good pet for the busy woman. Other than that killer bee variety, most are low-maintenance and unassuming creatures. If you mistakenly abuse them verbally or otherwise, they won't hold it against you. They are secure creatures and much too busy to notice your offending remarks.

My bees are always teaching me important things. For instance, I have learned that there is a natural order to the universe. Bees work hard, and they don't tolerate freeloaders. Order reigns when every bee-sister carries her load. Order is soothing to people and to bees. Order only comes about when everyone does their job.

The order in a bee hive is established by the presence of the Queen. And in every hive there is only one queen. This girlfriend will lay 1500 bee eggs a day (whoa, mama, whoa!) for about two years. She deserves a bit of domestic help, I think. Her noble birth predestines her to an exhausting occupation.

The Queen employs maids, groundskeepers, cooks, and nannies. Lots of them too. In my new hive, the Queen has nine thousand nine hundred ninety-nine domestic helpers.

A succession of no-nonsense workers, called nurse bees, give up the first twenty days of their short lives to keep the family humming along. They are like the nannies applying for work at the Banks household before Mary Poppins showed up. They are stern, focused nurses. They tend the larvae-babies, tidy up the bedrooms, and prepare meals for Queen and her husbands, the drones.

Drones, the male bees in the hive, are interesting additions to the home. They are incapable of feeding or caring for themselves. They wander aimlessly around the hive looking for someone to feed them and take care of their needs. Drones exist only to procreate with the Queen, and they die for this honor. Hmmmm. No parallels are being drawn here to the Homo sapiens family, just an interesting note. . . .

In the last half of their lives, nanny/nurse bees turn in their aprons for business suits and become field bees. They go off to forage the world for hive food. Their new job is to bring in the pollen. Day after day, until they die, they shuffle off to work. Every bee has a job and every bee does her job or she is foisted out of the hive and left to die in the grass. It is the natural order of things.

Human hive homes have a natural order to them as well. I learned this important lesson recently when I, Queen Busy Bee, was spiraling out of control in the final hours of an overcommitted week when my hive fell apart. Disorder and turmoil reigned. Bedtime for the larvae came and went. Nothing was on the stove (or in the oven) for dinner because I was trying to be worker bee to the world.

My husband, though not usually dronish, and our three larvae sat at the table looking emaciated and drawn as I buzzed around the

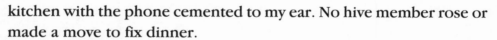

kitchen with the phone cemented to my ear. No hive member rose or made a move to fix dinner.

Swarming can occasionally occur when hive members are not happy with their living conditions. Swarming would have been O.K. with me just then. *Let those unhappy little bees pack their bags and leave en masse to another wax house,* I thought. *Better yet, let* me *swarm to a new, tidy hive.*

But they didn't swarm. They stayed put and they stared at me.

My drone is a capable man. He is a natural caretaker. But there he sat. Doing nothing but staring at me. *I think he misses me, his queen busy bee,* I said to myself.

Actually, all the hive members were very capable of flying off to fetch a nice pollen dinner for themselves. They didn't. They sat dispiritedly as I yammered on the phone. *They all miss me, even though I'm here, they miss me.* The little larvae and the drone wanted me to care for them the way I had been caring for stranger bees outside the hive, fussing over every detail of the foreign bees' lives.

They didn't say any of this with words. Everything was said in the sad, disconnected way they hummed around me and attached themselves to the hive. A Queen has the ability to sense the true meaning in the flight patterns of her hive members.

Everybody has a job in the hive. If the worker bee quits pulling in pollen, the brood will starve. If the nurse bees don't tidy things up, the larvae rot. And if the Queen starts fussing over foreign bees, neglecting her own hive, the whole colony goes berserk and falls apart. I used to think this was a sexist thing. Bees, though, are not sexist. They seem to know important things about taking care of their own.

I am always learning from my bees.■

—CW

SHARING YOUR SPACE

Airplane etiquette in the United States demands that a passenger *never* take a seat on the plane within touching distance of another passenger—if it possibly can be avoided. Emotional cooties might be transferred. Talking might happen—and then who knows what?

This is why I became annoyed with the man who fastened his happy self into the empty seat next to me on the flight to Vancouver.

Either he is a foreigner or he wants me, I thought.

My pile of reading material was supposed to ride in that empty seat. *The plane is half empty. Why me?*

I decided to punish the man for breaking the rule. I would not speak to him or look at him the whole flight. I read my book through the push-back. I read through the takeoff roll. I read through the ascent. I read until dinner. However, I am not coordinated enough to eat *and* pick bones out of a salmon carcass at the same time, so I had to put the book down. The rude man saw his opening.

"The fish is surprisingly delicious," he said, obviously wanting to be my friend.

"Yes," I said, stabbing at the plate. I didn't need any friends. Mothers don't need friends when they travel. Mothers need to be left alone.

"Interesting book you are reading," he tried again without a hint of shame.

"Mmm," I mumbled, pretending to have a mouthful.

"The cover is so interesting." *Oh brother, this guy was not going to give up.* He was missing all the overt clues in my antisocial behavior.

I looked at him—sized him up. He was not the kind to give up easily. So I did. I put my fork down and I gave up. *What's one more needy person in my life, bleeding me dry?*

We began to chat, first about the book I was reading, then about children and life. We hashed out the simple politics of our respective countries (he was foreign and didn't want me).

I became the one blabbering for more minutes than was polite. He folded his napkin on his dessert plate, listening intently to my profound theories on the life of a sect of nomadic women I was reading about.

He then shared a painful tale about his search for God and how, when he found God, his human father rejected him permanently. We swapped family stories, pictures, and dreams—my dream to write and his to be reunited with his dad. On it went until we rolled into the arrival gate.

He stood as I continued to blather on in dizzying trails of unfinished thought.

He handed me his card and said, "I think one day, you will write a book. But you are like the woman on the cover of the book you are reading. You are hiding behind a veil, afraid. Dream big. God's plans

are wilder than you could ever imagine. I'm sure I will one day see your name again. We will surely meet again on the other side of this life. I enjoyed sharing your space."

Enjoyed sharing your space. I embarrass myself sometimes. God wants to drop an angel of encouragement in my lap—and I snort like a mad pig at the prospect. I establish boundaries so extreme that I'm sure I've got the title "God's Major Grace Case" in heaven.

Enjoyed sharing your space. How many times has God wanted to perform some little wonderment for my antisocial self? How many times have I missed the wonderment simply because I won't consent to sharing my space? I am so routinely caught up short with the realization of how often I thwart the attempts of God as he tries to send happy tidings my way. The only thing he asks from me is to stay open to the opportunity—to share my space. ■

—CW

JUNK PIECE

In our casual, Florida beach town, where priests have been known to wear white bermuda shorts and black clerical collars, there is an Episcopal church that is hard not to notice as you drive by. A lighted cross shines from behind the altar through the glass doors and into the street. A second cross hangs outside on the face of the building.

If you go inside the church, you'll see a third cross: a heavy, brass cross. It is the processional cross: every Sunday morning it is held high on a pole and brought down the aisle. Ornately carved, it is exquisite in design.

It is that third brass cross that has a particularly remarkable story behind it. Theodore Jacobs, a man in his sixties, saw the brass cross for the first time while visiting his ailing mother in New York. "Jake," as his friends called him, was a photographer by trade. And wherever he traveled, he made it his practice to hunt for antique cameras.

While strolling the New York streets one steamy day, he was beckoned by the smell of old, dusty artifacts. He walked into an amusing-looking junk shop as much for cooling off as for shopping.

No cameras, he noted, but a tarnished, green cross lay half-buried under piles of old, discarded rejects. The shop was too dark to allow him a good look. Jake thought the cross looked remarkably like

the one he remembered being carried down the aisle during high mass in the big New York church he was raised in.

Jake left the shop and soon returned to Florida, giving that cross at the bottom of the pile in the store corner no more thought.

Two years later, on one of his final trips to see his dying mother, he saw the cross again. It rested exactly where he last saw it—in the same old, musty store, sandwiched between the unwanted has-beens of life in a forgotten corner of the room.

Jake dug away at the rubbish and artifacts until he could yank the cross free. The intricately carved letters and symbols looked distinctive and important and were like that cross of his childhood church. He carried it into the light. It felt so heavy in his arms. A dull, green tarnish obscured his assessment of the metal. *Maybe valuable, maybe not,* Jake thought. *A gamble to be sure, but if it polished up nice, it would be a great gift for my pastor—he loves crosses.*

Jake haggled with the shop owner. "Eighty-five dollars, firm," the man said.

"Too much," Jake countered.

"Cheap!" replied the owner.

Jake bought the cross for seventy dollars. He walked out into the sunshine feeling good about his purchase. He carried the piece over to the city church. The priest there said it was a real find and Jake was lucky to get it for only seventy dollars. As Jake had thought, this cross was nearly identical to the city-church cross, which cost thousands. Jake's cross, however, was older—even more valuable.

Jake loaded the cross into his car and drove it back to Florida.

This cross, he knew, might be worth thousands of dollars. But for Jake, its monetary value was only a shadow of its true meaning, just as the dullness and age of the cross were simply a covering for the shiny surface beneath. It was the hidden value of that cross that meant something real to him, meant something about the *real* cross and the *real* God-man who hung on that cross.

Jake paid a small amount for a valuable thing. This Jesus spent everything he had; he paid the *high* price.

Back home in his Episcopal church, Jake presented the cross, flawless and gleaming, to the priest. The church mounted it on a staff.

Now on Sundays, the crucifer carries the cross down the center aisle, lifted high. Everyone in the church can see the shiny, brass glory piece. Some let it pass without a thought. Others, like Jake, know the real story. They know its worth and that the cross didn't come cheap. It is, in fact, a rare and priceless treasure.■

—KB

SARAH'S STORY PARAPHRASED

Sarah was married to that old patriarch Abraham. Abe was a dreamer—not an easy man to live with. One day he said to Sarah, "Honey, I think we're going to move."

"O.K., cool," she said. "Let's pick up this tent and go."

"Hon," he told her, "we're going to leave our family and the property in Ur and try it over there in Canaan."

"O.K. Abe. I love ya, so let's go," she said.

So Abe and Sarah, off they went. On the way to Canaan, Abe made a bad mistake. He decided to stop over in Egypt, a nasty land with an even nastier king. Abe looked at his darling Sarah and said, "Honey, we are in a pickle. You are so beautiful. You'll have to lie to the king and say you're my sister. Otherwise, Baby, they might try to kill me so they can have you—you know how it goes with evil kings. But if you say you're my sister, they might kind of feast on you instead of me and ya, ya, ya . . . " On he droned with his special line of logic. No one knew what that man was thinking, least of all Sarah.

Sarah really loved this guy. So she lied for him. The next thing she knew, the king's servants were primping and powdering and preparing her for the evil king. Sarah was not happy about this. She didn't feel real close or lovey-dovey with Abe. She started thinking, *I don't like the way this scene is playing out. In fact, I'm getting down-*

right hacked off. How could this happen? Except for a few slip-ups, I'm a godly woman.

No one knows exactly what Sarah was thinking, of course. My guess is she wanted to murder the guy. *He got me into this mess. Moved me from my home. My family was there. I loved my family. They loved me. I didn't have to be here. Look at me now! I'm over here in this strange land, and they are dolling me up for some creep who's planning to abuse me.*

But God showed up for Sarah. He knew what was going on. He dumped serious disease on the king and his house because the king was keeping Sarah there. And God told the king that Sarah was someone else's babe. The king then said to Abe, "What's the matter with you, man? Why didn't you tell me this babe was your wife? Take her and *go!*" Abe got his wife out of there lickety-split and pressed on for the land of Canaan.

Twenty-some years later, God showed up again for Sarah. He gave her something she'd been wanting for *seventy years.* God said to her, "Hey, Sarah, you're going to have a baby." Now Sarah knew that God came through for her in hard times, but she had a long history of faith troubles in the baby area.

She laughed at God. "Yeah, right," she said. "At ninety? Sure. Am I going to have sex with Abraham? He's a hundred. I don't think so."

Then a little while later, at the birth of her baby, old, wrinkly Sarah laughed again. This was the kind of laughing she had never done before, this was a different thing. "Look at me!" she said to anyone who would listen, "I'm ninety. I laughed at God. Still, He showed up.

He gave me this baby just like he promised. I think I'll name him Isaac—it means *laughter*. My Isaac, he is the promise of God. A promise given to me, even though I laughed."

After that, when anyone who would ask her how she could believe in God in the middle of difficult situations, Sarah would say, "I've seen God show up. I've seen him show up when I cried in the house of a kooky king. I've seen him show up to keep me married all these years to that dreamer, Abe. I've seen God show up after years of my crying about being childless.

"He gave me faith to believe the promise would come. Now I laugh. And I have a son of laughter because God showed up. Smile, laugh with me."■

—KB

MY JEALOUSY

I was a new mother. I had a friend who was a new mother too. She was elegant. I was not. Women who are bloated and hormonal should *not* hang out with elegant friends. While battling post-partum acne, emotional despair, and a body the size of a market hog, new mothers had best forget any icons of worldly glory for a while.

My friend (pretend her name is Olivia) gave birth to one perfectly pink baby girl. I, a woman with no discernible torso, proceeded to deliver, not babies really, but partially grown toddlers the size of beach balls.

Olivia was always dressed to the nines. And her little girl was always dressed to the thirteens. I never, ever, saw Olivia without lipstick or foundation. Rumor had it she vacuumed the tracks in her carpet after anyone walked through her living room. She was perfect.

The worst part was, Olivia was the proud owner of a body like the Venus de Milo with arms. I pretended not to notice or care when I was with her, but behind her back, I was so jealous I could spit.

When I finished having babies I wanted desperately to look like Olivia—she had a waistline. I just had a line between two rolls of flab that sat on top of each other (picture bagel dough with a crease in the middle, and you've got the idea).

When Olivia came home from the hospital she was wearing her pre-maternity jeans. Worse than that—she could zip them up. I

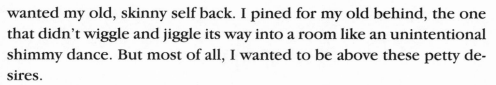

wanted my old, skinny self back. I pined for my old behind, the one that didn't wiggle and jiggle its way into a room like an unintentional shimmy dance. But most of all, I wanted to be above these petty desires.

My friendship with Olivia, historically, did not boast great depth, but it had its pleasantries. We could talk about anything so long as it was "pleasant." Italian shoes, designer clothes, home furnishings, and travel were spicy topics. Religion, politics, and feelings were *verboten.* That didn't trouble me. I was in counseling at the time. I engaged in one too many deep conversations with the potted palm in Dr. Dave's office as it was. I longed to hang around like the old days and talk about shallow things knowing I was really a very deep person inside.

As one might expect, a nasty bend occurred in our relationship because of my out-of-control envy. We both knew something was wrong, and we both knew that something was *me.* The terrible truth was, I sensed pain behind all her glitzy glamour from the beginning, but I was too self-absorbed to do anything about it. Sitting across the counter from each other droning on about silk scarves and De Haviland china, sadness would come over me. Quickly I brushed it away and got busy with my fat feelings or my jealousy feelings. Soon I could forget I saw sadness in her soul and get back to concentrating on me, myself, and I.

The pain of my comparisons finally drove us apart. I didn't see Olivia for a long time. Recently we turned up at the same soiree. Olivia was surrounded by a gaggle of post-birth women aching to look like her, be like her. I felt sorry for all of us. Sorry for Olivia, because she was admired for biology she couldn't control much longer—and the rest of us for thinking biology was *It*.

Olivia and I connected in the middle of the room when the gaggle dispersed. After a lengthy discussion about the duck pâté, English antiques, and Aspen, I asked after her husband and daughter. She hinted there was trouble of the marital variety.

Some growing up occurred in my life over the years—having worked through some painful things myself and having found a good source of help, I thought to mention my best friend, God. Bristly air came between us. Olivia's eyes turned blacker than the sevruga caviar. She rattled off a few disconnected thoughts about "the circle of life" and departed lickety-split, throwing an atmospheric kiss in my direction.

A huge pocket of sad air filled up the space after she left. A waiter handed me the cocktail Olivia ordered before she dashed off. I set it down on the table. Too sad to eat or drink anymore, I went home.

The sad air followed me around for a few days. I mailed a "pleasant note" to Olivia. But this my-best-friend-God stuff kept leaking out onto the page. I tried to hide it. But you can't hide something that has become so big in your life.

Olivia never answered my mail. I am still sorry and still sad. Jealousy is a terrible thing; it wastes time and keeps depth from happening in a friendship.

I have something important to say, something that might help my friend, but she isn't listening. She isn't listening because for too

many years I talked about shoes and crab dip, and ignored my-best-friend-God. I made Olivia's perfectness my god.

I have something to say now.

—CW

SHEEP STRESS

One thing the world needs more of is stress. But if we don't have enough stress already, we can make it up: *imagined stress*. My friend Marilyn had a sheep once who did that. He made up stress.

Marilyn and her husband, Crum, own a farm and a small herd of sheep. Normally, the fifteen sheep travel around the pasture, nose to tail, tail to nose, the way sheep are wont to do. Up and down and all around, they rove the grounds like one big, woolly machine. One particular little sheep, "Sam" we'll call him, followed his passel of fellow sheep around faithfully.

One morning Marilyn noticed only fourteen moving parts to the machine. Number fifteen—Sam—lagged several sheep lengths behind the rest. To sheep behaviorists, this is a bad sign. Sam was dragging his little sheep leg behind him. A twisty piece of barbed wire wound around his rear flank and hooked into his knotty wool. The more he tried to untangle himself, the more tangled and stuck he became.

Shepherd Crum (Marilyn's husband) made valiant attempts to grab the little lamb, hoping to free his leg from the fencing. But he—the sheep, not Marilyn's husband—freaked out.

"Nooo, let meee go," he bleated. "Don't help meee. I'll manage

all alone." Well, of course, Sam-the-lamb didn't really say this. But he looked like he wanted to.

Snip, snip, snip. The wires were finally cut and the lamb turned loose. No damage to the leg, thankfully.

You're free, baby. Go! Run away. Shoo!

But Sam couldn't stop imagining he still had stress. He hobbled away, holding his leg in that funny position as if that barbed wire was still snagging him. All day long, Sam dragged himself around thinking he was still ensnared by that dastardly wire. *Run away, little lamb. Jump! Go! Nothing's wrong with you anymore.* He couldn't get over it. He couldn't stop imagining he had this stressful piece of wire holding him captive.

Stress is not healthy for a sheep or a person. We all have enough to worry about without conjuring up imaginary stress. Imagined stress is always far worse than the real thing. Barbed wire wrapped around your leg is a bad thing. But *imaginary* barbed wire can snake right up to your throat and choke the life right out of you.

My imaginary barbed wire always trails down frightening alleys in my mind. As a new mother, I worried about all kinds of crazy stuff that might be happening to my baby. Once I wandered off into one of these alleys thinking about what might happen if Baby caught a cold. A respiratory illness would make it difficult for Baby to breathe. If she couldn't breathe, she couldn't take her bottle. If she couldn't take her bottle, she would lose weight. If she lost weight, one of two horrible things would happen: A) the baby would starve to death or B) she would lose sufficient weight as to alarm the authorities. The authorities would take her from my care, putting me in jail, where I would go completely berserk from losing my baby.

These unchecked thoughts running wild are imagined stress. They are always worse than the real thing. This is why there is an important saying in the Bible that tells us not to give in to crazy thinking. It says, "Take captive every thought." Put your leg down and say, *"Stop!* I will no longer tolerate this imaginary barbed wire handicapping my life. This pasture I live in has enough real barbed wire to worry about. And it probably won't do half the scary things the imaginary wire will do." Put your leg down before that wire snakes right up to your throat. *Flick your leg. Go! Jump! Run! Be free, baby! Shoo!* ■

—CW

81

3

The Red-Hot Blue Plate Special

Stories about the Love Thing

W herever you go, there you are. And dragging behind you is a whole satchel full of fancy notions about love that need to be thrown out. They need to be thrown out because they are notions based on years of distorted rumor and plain old fiction. They need to be thrown out because they are somebody else's ideas about affection. You will be left sad and alone in life holding a bag of love ideas that don't belong to you. It was not your *Blue Plate Special*.

God thought up the idea of love. He made it simple. He made it universal.

"Love everybody the way you love yourself," he said. We got it all tangled up with sex and stirred in some conditional things like, "—only if there is something in it for me."

We made God's sentence longer than it needed to be. We confused ourselves in the process.

Love happens every day, like the Blue Plate Special. One day it's roast turkey with gravy, dessert included. Sometimes there is no dessert. There seems to be no reward for cleaning your plate. There is always the freedom to choose another meal, but generally the Special is the best way to go. You get the most for your

money with the Blue Plate Special. And God made it up special just that day.

86

THE SCALLOP MAN

I am serene—positively June Cleaverish—about this, my third excursion today, to the grocery store. One more time. Just me and the three children roaming the aisles for those already twice-overlooked items.

"Forgot the fish for tonight's dinner," I say with only slightly clenched teeth.

The cheery fishmonger is absent this day. The meat man—who knows next to nothing about fish—saunters over to assist me. He only does this after a lengthy internal debate over whether or not it is his job to help me.

"Do you have any sea scallops?" I ask sweetly, smiling a really big Christian smile so all my teeth show.

He points wordlessly to the bay scallops.

"Those are *bay* scallops," I tell him, still smiling big. He rolls his eyeballs up into his hairline and gives me that you-are-a-stupid-bimbo-housewife-and-you-need-to-get-a-life look. I hate that look.

"I don't like bay scallops, their smallness creeps me out," I say, trying to make him smile.

The meat man does not think I'm funny. He glares at my children, who are now pulling each other's hair, and I feel June Cleaver departing and another, less attractive person taking over—it's Cujo, the Mad-Dog Mother. I begin to froth at the mouth and my fangs pop out.

"The fruit of the Spirit is lovejoypeacepatiencekindnessgoodness selfcontrol. . . . " I mumble really fast so I won't say a bad word in front of my kids.

"They swim from the bay into the sea and back again," he says as I am frantically reciting my verse over and over. "Trust me, Hon," he says, "these were caught in the sea."

I hate being called "Hon." I am beginning to dislike this man very much.

I wonder, *Do I have to be nice to this gas-bag, Lord? Do you really love this condescending creep? More importantly, do I have to love this creep?* I don't say this out loud because I want my children to be better people than I am.

"Listen, Sir," I say. —O.K., so I did not say "Sir." Maybe I said, "Listen, Pal" or "Buddy-boy." I wanted to say, "Listen, Jerk, the *real* fish guy knows the difference between a *sea* scallop and a *bay* scallop, and he would never try to demean a haggard, pitiful, worn-to-a-fraz mother."

But of course I don't have the guts to say any of this. I simply do an internal broil and quietly loathe him.

Internal broils make you twitch funny, and loathing makes your face turn weird colors. So of course *it* happens: I pitch a fit right there in front of all the swordfish kebobs and the headless salmon reclining on comfy beds of kale. I snort away scallopless, muttering under my breath, knowing full well I am making an absolute fool out of myself over crustaceans—over slimy, beige balls.

I can't get a grip on the eternity thing just then. I can't figure out why Jesus would love a mean old man who takes sport in harassing a sweet June Cleaver-ish person like myself.

"Are you praying, Mommy?" the little people in the cart ask me as they study my wordless, moving lips. "Don't you like that man, Mommy? What about the scallops, Mommy?"

"Forget about the scallops!" I say with my Christian teeth clenched tight.

What I really mean is, "Forget about the scallop man. I don't like this scallop man. I want to get away from this scallop man." And then this verse begins to rattle around in my brain:

> *I do not understand what I am doing;*
> *I am not practicing what I would like to do;*
> *I am doing the very thing I hate—*
> *for the sake of slimy beige balls.* (Chris Wave 1:1)

That's not exactly how it is in the Bible, but that is how I feel.

Scallops schmallops. This is not about the fish I wanted to have for dinner. It is about how hard it is to love someone who is not lovable. This story is about how lucky we are that God is in charge of the Love Department and not me. I dole out love conditionally and only to those who merit it. God pours out buckets of love indiscriminately on crabby scallop men and testy little mothers even when we don't deserve it. ■

— CW

CAR TROUBLE

The old woman's gloveless hands clutched the grocery cart as she steered into the icy wind. The cart wobbled and stalled crossing the rails of the empty train tracks. Snow fell in thick chunks, blotting out the afternoon sun. She was a painful sight against the inclemency of the day.

Oblivious to the angry honkings of speeding cars, she pushed her cart straight into the heart of traffic, aiming for a thin median dividing the lanes. The median tapered to nothing in less than a hundred feet. It had all the earmarks of a suicide mission.

I didn't really have time to help her. I was already late for the carpool pickup. But the image of her peril refused to let me pass on.

"I'd like to give you a ride," I called as I pulled alongside her. Angry commuters protested the delay with screeching tires and blaring horns. The old woman said nothing. "Please get in. I'll load your groceries." Still, she said nothing. Her eyes, piercing and nervous, conveyed no hint of understanding. Her gaze darted suspiciously all around but never once met my eyes.

Coming to a stop ahead of her, I slid the van door open. She grasped the seat back, her hands turned whitish with the struggle to pull herself in. Most of the fingers on her right hand ended after the first joint. Thick scars covered the stubs like band-aids made of flesh.

I tried to fasten the seat belt around her waist. An angry, gutteral sound came from her lungs in protest. I backed away, startled by the noise, which sounded more like an animal in distress than a human being.

"Where do you live?" I asked as I signaled my way back into the traffic. She said nothing. The woman's suspicious, darting glances alarmed my children in the rear seat.

"Mom?" my daughter called from the back, needing reassurance that she and her brother were safe.

"I'm just going to pick up my other daughter from school." I tried to sound soothing. "Then we'll find out where you live."

A wild snorting, similar to the noise made over the seat belt, erupted again. Only now it was more vicious, more desperate. My heart raced. What about my waiting child? What about the two seated in back? What kind of jeopardy might I have put us all in?

Her noises were so frightening I obediently passed the school where my child waited. I drove straight ahead until she signaled me to do otherwise. Frantic rappings on the back window with her fingerless hand told me to turn right. Angry, snorting noises said, "You've done something wrong."

Eight miles from the place I'd first seen her, we turned into a frozen, rutted driveway. A badly decaying relic from decades past served as home. A child's rusty tricycle was tipped on its side and held comatose in the compacted snow. The metal storm door banged wildly against its frame. Dozens of black, plastic garbage bags posed like eerie frozen statues in the snow-covered yard.

The woman hunched her angular frame into the wind. She

watched with piercing intensity as I carried her groceries to the door. Before I reached my car again, she slammed the metal door shut without a word.

This good deed didn't feel so good. What was I looking for? A thank-you from a woman unable to even tell me where she lived? A pat on the back? An "atta girl"?

Love is often untidy. Real love, not Hollywood fluff stuff. It is firm, unchangeable, and hard. It is often missing that feel-good quality we human beings are perennially on the prowl for. Real love isn't tidy. In fact it's downright messy. Real love doesn't pass by the unlovely in pain. Real love doesn't look for a thank-you. It is its own reward.

Jesus loved a man who would eventually sell him out for a bit of silver. He loved him as much as the other eleven who didn't sell him out. He loved the Pharisees enough to tell them the truth about their spiritual condition. He said, You are like whitewashed tombs, looking good on the outside but filled with a bunch of rattly bones on the inside.

Jesus loved two violent, demon-possessed men who caused others to turn aside in fear and disgust. He loved a lonely, old woman missing some fingers and probably a tongue by sending her help in a blizzard. He loved a common mother of three enough to show her what real love is.■

—CW

LOVE SOUP

When someone I love is sad, I make soup. Nothing thaws melancholia like broth and love. I pay no attention to intricate soup rules requiring hours of preparation and scads of forethought. I've little time for making fancy French spice balls or stock from roasted chickens. But I have time enough for love, given in the form of a simple soup.

So it was that when my friend was in pain, I made soup. I combined the last remaining ingredients in my near-empty, winter cupboard and ended up with alchemy. Days later, my friend called, raving endlessly about my soup and begging for the recipe. I, being a distracted mother of three, had forgotten I'd even made the soup. And I spent the next few days trying to re-create the beloved broth to her satisfaction.

"No, that's not it!" She'd shake her head with every combination of ingredients I suggested. I verbally cooked and re-cooked the soup until I was sick of the whole event. Then I finally figured it out. It was the *love* that made the difference. I kept forgetting to tell her about the love.

The following recipe (though I believe it to be greatly enhanced over the original version) met with her final, grudging approval.

1 lb. spicy vegetarian chorizo
4 cans unsalted chicken broth
1 diced onion
2 cans any bean on your shelf
1 28-oz. can peeled tomatoes, chopped
1 big dash of love

Combine all ingredients. Heat thoroughly. If you plopped the sausage in frozen (as I did) this will take 30 minutes. That's it. Really! If your friend whines, as mine did, insisting the recipe be more complicated, write out the following directions:

Early in the morning before you've had your coffee or fed your family, begin your homemade chicken stock by slow roasting a free-range, organically-fed, young hen. Crush four hundred dollars' worth of imported spices with a marble mortar and pestle. Add the ingredients in the order you placed them in your grocery cart. Stop after each spice addition to stir fifty times. Cook all day over a flame tamer. Do not leave the stove for even a nanosecond. Taste-test the broth every sixty seconds.

This whole process prior to consumption should take 23½ hours.

Or you could add love and save 23 hours. ■

—CW

GOD IN THE DISGUSTING LINE

Perched like an I-beam between two grocery carts, I shuffled down the store aisles an arm's length from any child I'd given birth to. In one cart sat the baby, miraculously still, with both lower extremities staying in the appropriate leg slots. In the basket of that same cart, the middle child played with the uncrushables. The other cart, containing the squishable groceries, was being pulled forward by the oldest child.

I looked pretty good this day—if you were standing four lanes away. Closer up the picture was not so attractive. A cement-like paste of partially digested cookie encrusted my left shoulder. Clumps of over-sprayed, not-recently-washed hair unglued themselves from the hundred-pin *chignon* that I hastily arranged on my head. Flailing, loose clumps of hair sprouted new creations of their own design. There were now many hairdos on my one head.

Behind us in line stood a meticulously groomed woman in an elegant red suit. Perfectly manicured nails matched perfectly polished pumps. No milky stains marred those pumps. I was certain that under her perfectly tinted and coifed hair was a brain that could complete a sentence.

The perfect person smiled sweetly at my son, melting all my bad feelings.

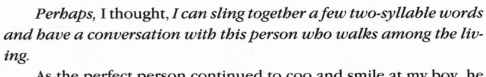

Perhaps, I thought, *I can sling together a few two-syllable words and have a conversation with this person who walks among the living.*

As the perfect person continued to coo and smile at my boy, he let loose with a sneeze that rocked all of northern Illinois. I didn't need to look at him to know there were sneeze remnants all over his face—I could tell by the look on the woman's face.

"Don't look!" I said to her as I groped in my purse for a tissue. As usual, the black hole in my purse had swallowed anything with the slightest absorbency. Then I did what every tissue-less mother has done at least once in her life: I wiped his nose with my hand then wiped my hand on my jeans.

The perfect woman walked away to a less disgusting line.

My life is chock full of humiliating moments that defy escape or reason. God has a funny sense of humor. He uses my children to tell all the world that I am not as perfect as I pretend to be. As I am busy wrenching around to pat myself on the back, my kids slink about playing accountability police.

"Mom! Are you hiding from Mrs. So-and-So?" they ask as I pretend not to see a woman who has been needy lately.

"Mom! The cashier gave you too much of a discount!" says the math genius.

"Mom, is that really true?" I hear after I've embellished yet another story.

The good news for me is Jesus is not surprised by my behavior. He expects it. Still he loves me. In the Bible it says that he actually *de-*

lights in me. Imagine that. The Bible also says he doesn't run away from the disgusting lines. Jesus is no wimp. He is willing to hang out in the not-so-clean or pretty lines, like mine. He holds my hand—and probably he would even hold the dirty tissue.■

—CW

THE LOVE GIG

There are two types of people in this world. The first are Chuggers, those who chug down the universe—swallowing life in one big fast and furious gulp—and suffer unbearable indigestion for it. And the other people: Fretters and Worriers, those who percolate and ruminate so long over the minute particles of life that they never actually get to eat anything at all.

God thinks it's funny to match these extreme types in matrimony. He does this to create marital friction, because friction breeds pain and builds character. And a strong-tempered character is necessary to make real love happen.

I am wed to a percolator. This man can question, reason, rationalize, scrutinize, sift through, study, survey, strategize, synthesize, and probe any subject to death. He once spent three years researching fax machines. He called Tony in Florida, Brian in Virginia, Marty, Al, Fred, Joe, and Sam.

"What kind of fax machine do you have?" he would ask the prepubescent sales clerk at Safe Buy.

"Egad!" I screamed at him. "Just do it! Say *YES* to life! Take a risk! Walk on the wild side! Hop on the bus, Gus! Buy any stupid fax machine on the shelf. This is *not* surgery on your child's cranium! I would rather poke my finger in my eye than shop with you one more day for a sixty-four-dollar-and-ninety-nine-cent machine. And if you continue to torture me by not getting that stupid thing soon, I just may cut you off from some of life's little pleasures."

I've got to say that "cut you off" thing always works with men. He bought a fax machine.

Another grand-scale survey soon was conducted. Over ear piercing. My husband called the father of every friend our daughter knew to discuss the pros and cons of a hole the size of a flea dropping.

"Hey, Jim, John, Randy, Bill, Tom: Does your daughter . . . ?" For eons he made our poor girl twitch and writhe in the agony of anticipation while he pro-ed and con-ed this issue to death.

This ability he has to think before he acts held great attraction for me when I met him. Today, however, I can tell you that that man and his perpetual percolation drive me to prayer. When I hear him say, "I need to look into *(fill in the blank)* further," I run to my closet and lock the door. I pray until God unclenches my fists. I pray fervent prayers. I pray until the sweat runs. I pray until the electronics of my nervous system stop firing sparks. I pray until I don't want to hurt him anymore.

Of course, he believes he is the rock, the stable rudder in the shifting waves of my ever-changing whims. He sees me chasing after new ideas and feels that being married to me is like herding a husk of wild hares.

One day I'm in the horse-trading business, the next I'm dispensing herbal-remedy advice like Granny Clampett. Last year alone, I cooked up so many get-rich-quick schemes that I left him spinning

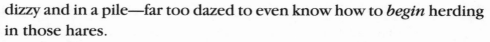

dizzy and in a pile—far too dazed to even know how to *begin* herding in those hares.

My husband's heart begins to beat erratically and he waxes pale every time he hears me say, "I have an idea." He usually runs to his office and locks the door.

One time a man with an advanced counseling degree asked him, "Do you sometimes think that marrying her is the greatest mistake you've ever made?" My poor husband heaved an elephant-sized sigh that sucked all the air out from between his ribs. He slumped pitifully in his chair.

"Yes," he said. He looked quickly to see if he'd hurt my feelings. Which of course he hadn't, because I wasn't listening—I was trying to figure out how to keep free-range Buff Orphington chickens in the back yard.

This is how it goes with love. You are in for disappointment if you think otherwise. The interesting affectation that draws you to that handsome date is the very thing that drives you nuts later on.

After the lust gig is up, the marriage gig moves in. Early on we believe we've been doing the love thing, because it feels so good. Suddenly, though, it stops feeling so good. All that friction and chafing starts up; and it begins to look a lot like serious incompatibility. We get all bumfuzzled and think we lost the love. When we start getting to know each other—really know each other—the "feel good" stuff gets all twisted up in a gnarly ball of angst.

If we don't faint dead away at the first sign of discomfort, a mysterious transmuting occurs. Real love happens. The bad news is, real love doesn't show up before that discomfort thing happens. It arrives on the heels of the nagging feeling, "Oh my, this person is the greatest mistake I've made thus far in my life. This doesn't feel good anymore and I want out." That's about where it starts.

Maybe we need a new word for the gobbledygook masquerading around the universe as *love*. Maybe we should call it *lerk*. We could say for instance, "I'm in lerk right now, because it still feels good."

Lerk is good. We need not dispense with it. Lerk *must* happen before love. But that love gig is what's worth it all: worth the wait, worth the work, worth getting to know each other, worth getting de-lerked. The love gig is about surety. It is knowing that hard winds will be heading in your direction, they always do. Those winds can blow all they want. Love doesn't mind, because love doesn't let the difficulties come between you and the one you love. *Love* is the glue. *Lerk,* on the other hand, just isn't glue-ey at all. It's not strong enough to hold people together. It hasn't been around long enough to develop tenacity. It wasn't meant to.

So, if you are being driven crazy and are experiencing a measure of discomfort, be happy. God is allowing the lerk to wear away, and in its place is that glue-ey, forever stuff called *love.*

—CW

SOMEBODY ELSE'S SON

My folks and Tony and I were enjoying an after-dinner coffee. The evening news was over, and we all commented about the war in Kosovo: how young the soldiers were; how unfair war was to everyone, on both sides. In response, my dad began to reminisce about life as a soldier in World War II.

He was barely sixteen. To lie about his age then seemed right. This was for his country. He was a soldier now. A man. The orders read: "Raid farmhouse along the border for German soldiers. Leave no corner unturned."

Five jeeps carrying American soldiers roared up to a humble, white farmhouse in the middle of the night. The soldiers pushed and shoved their way through the door. The fearsome weapons they carried made each command more powerful. The American soldiers shouted rude, rough commands. The frightened family understood. Even though the words were foreign, the angry shoving and the guns spoke clearly.

Satisfied that no enemy soldiers were stowed away in the home, the soldiers roared up their jeep engines and raced off into the black night, leaving only tracks in the snow.

But the last jeep in the lineup stalled in the yard, frozen in the snow. Despite frantic, repeated efforts by the young soldier, the engine failed to start. The boy's blood pounded inside his head. Nothing he tried would turn the engine over. It strained and sputtered in the cold night air until finally, it completely stalled into silence. Stranded at the German border, sitting in front of the house he had just raided with comrades a moment ago, the boy felt his full age, sixteen. Never before had he felt so alone.

Why don't the guys look back to see if I am with them—to see if I got out? Will they notice I'm gone? Will they come back for me?

The farmhouse family peered out at the boy through a slit in the window curtains. Hours passed, it seemed, and the boy grew cold. The father came out of the house into the black night. He motioned for the soldier to come into the warmth of the house. The family looked on as the boy and the father walked in together.

The mother motioned for the soldier to sit at the table. She served him warm black bread with butter and hot soup. Out of her mother-heart she was able to see a boy, afraid, away from his family and homeland. Words were not, could not, be spoken—they would not have been understood. But appreciative nods and tentative smiles were passed between them.

The mother made up a bed for the boy, who marveled that the woman held no malice toward him. How quickly, how easily, it seemed to him, did she move beyond the pain of that aggressive raid against her family just hours earlier.

That night, his belly full, the young soldier slept well. The

mother probably didn't sleep. Probably she was a little afraid. But she did what mothers do. She didn't take in a soldier. She took in a son. Somebody else's son.

—KB

4

Child's Plate: Peanut Butter and Jelly Omelets

Stories about Life with Kids

Diners are usually pleasant enough places, unless you are a parent sitting off in the corner with an unruly infant or two. Childless diner patrons, observing your table decorations of cracker wrappers, wadded napkins, and peanut butter and jelly omelets, ask to be seated anywhere but your corner. Who could blame them? If we are honest, there are days we would rather be seated anywhere else as well.

Mothers and fathers spend long days wishing for the time they will once again commune with tall members of the human race—members whose eyebrows are not glued together with jelly blobs. We long for simple things. We long to go to the bathroom alone or to sleep three hours in a row.

Parenting is a difficult occupation. Sometimes the job is tedious and wearisome. Other times it feels surprisingly lonely. Most times, though, we parents would crawl over miles of broken glass for those little people. We would willingly hack up our lower extremities for the very ones who bring us so often to our knees in bafflement and despair. God knows this, and he uses these deep feelings to extract wonderful things from our character.

Parenting is God's great school of character development. His school employs the immersion theory. For long periods it seems like it's you, God, the kids, God, the kids, and you. God is mining for the fine traits like humility while teaching unconditional love.

The Child's Plate is never what you think it's going to be. It is a lot like eating in the mess hall of the military. It is boot camp food. Still, this is the dish that brings us closest to understanding the love of God, our parent.

His job is not easy. He sees us daily, really looks at us. Our runny noses and absurd, embarrassing ways would turn away the best of caretakers. God thinks we are too precious for words. Couldn't love us more. He would, in a heartbeat, crawl over broken glass for us, jelly blobs on our brow and all.

BAD AIR

Sometimes you can't do anything about bad air. This is particularly true about the air in vehicles shared with small children.

The first Fourth of July that my daughter Elyse could be called cognizant, she spent crying about "scary noises" in her daddy's arms. My husband was only too happy to retreat to the quietness of the car instead of warring with mosquitoes whose proboscises poked into every pore of exposed skin.

Our daughter was potty training at the time. Children are exceptionally fussy during this rite of passage. All the accouterment must be perfect during this time. For my daughter this meant that the car be closed, almost hermetically sealed, without a crack of air. Daddy could not move one micrometer from her hot, sticky side (even to empty the potty). And heaven forbid he open a window to banish those warm accumulating odors. So there they huddled for two hours. Father, daughter, and a potty chair. In the heat. In the van. With the windows rolled up. Her Daddy didn't mind. It was for love. This is what a dad does.

The second incidence of bad air occurred on a feverish August night. We were pressing the clock on our way north for our final summer camping trip. One hundred and twenty minutes remained until set-up prohibition hour. If we did not keep up a steady interstate

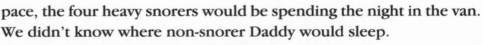

pace, the four heavy snorers would be spending the night in the van. We didn't know where non-snorer Daddy would sleep.

My boy suddenly and with persuasive urgency screamed out, "I have to use the potty *now!*"

There wasn't an exit for a few miles and we didn't have time to stop even if there was one.

We belted the little guy onto the purple and white plastic potty and continued with breakneck speed down I-90. There our son sat for an hour.

The odor was quite bad. Distressingly bad. It was a hundred and two degrees inside the car. And he was, for some reason, cold. We took turns cracking our windows wide enough to shove a nose through. If my son detected the minuscule crevice of air, he screamed.

"My ears are cold! I feel air on my ears!" The girls doubled over in the back seat making retching noises.

When finally he felt safe enough to come off the potty, I slid it out from under him only to discover it was too full to leave unattended as planned in the rearmost portion of the speeding vehicle. This did not mean good things for me as the only adult, responsible passenger not driving. Wordlessly and without a vote, I was appointed cup bearer. The warm potty would rest on my lap for the last hour of our journey. My husband looked as if he'd just been released from the East Peoria jail. I didn't say, *Why me?* I knew. This is what a parent does. This was for love.

The radiant heat of this August night cooked the ingredients of the potty chair for sixty long minutes. We reached the park ranger's station with seconds remaining in our set-up time. My husband and I looked at each other instantly reading each other's thought. Fear etched his brow. We had to open the window to speak to the ranger.

"Pray the man isn't downwind," my husband said.

As in every family, there is a story for *each* child. The last Bad Air Tale takes place on a fall night, again in the close confines of an automobile. This child was vomiting. After a prolonged two-hour crawl along the expressway in rush hour, we arrived at Auntie's for a weekend visit. My daughter raced into Auntie's house and threw up. Auntie blanched. I knew what she was thinking. The flu is an alarming illness in her home because she is skinny and her two little girls are skinny. A bout with the flu can leave them emaciated and looking as if they've lived through a lengthy famine.

Our weekend at Auntie's slid down the drain along with Lauren's flu. We climbed back into the car and picked our way home along the same stretch of highway, only now the cars were glued end to end and immobilized like live highway art.

Of course, as is the tendency in each of these stories, Lauren was cold. The heat was cranked so high my feet were roasting like two T-bones on a grill. I pulled off every piece of clothing I could without alerting authorities. Added to that was the smell. The plastic, gallon-sized baggy Auntie gave us was starting to look like an overblown balloon.

And, of course, Lauren was unable to bear a crack of air coming in the window. We stewed and simmered in the bad air for two hours.

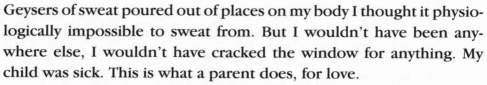

Geysers of sweat poured out of places on my body I thought it physiologically impossible to sweat from. But I wouldn't have been anywhere else, I wouldn't have cracked the window for anything. My child was sick. This is what a parent does, for love.

Planet Earth seems like it's become one big, overfilled potty sometimes. But never fear, God is with us. Why does he stay with us through the smelly mess? For love. That's what a parent does.

He stays in the car with us even with all our sickness and grime. Murder, rape, pillage, national ruin, child pornography. The world stinks. This is the potty chair God holds in his lap. The heat is on, but God's not sweating. There seems not to be a crack of good air anywhere in the world. But God is still breathing steady. This is what the parent of the world does. He loves the whole mess of us. Bad air doesn't change the love. He wishes we would get over our sickness and live healthy. He waits for us to ask for the medicine he offers. But in the meantime he's not bailing out. He's here to stay. Why? For love. That's what a parent does.■

—CW

DIAPERS AND THE FALL OF AMERICA

H ere is a trustworthy statement that Procter & Gamble needs to hear: The decline of modern civilization can be directly attributed to the diaper moguls of the United States.

Once upon a time, haggard mothers could be seen motoring off to The Joe Schmedlapp Grocery Store and picking up a sack of diapers in under ten minutes. Choosing a diaper with the best sticky tape was the only tricky part of the diaper quest. Any adult family member could be dispatched to the store for disposables simply by writing the word *diapers* on the shopping list.

A decade later that same note needed to read: *Please get Horst's brand, size medium, extra heavy wetters, night time, Tuesday edition, blue with primary-colored truckies on them.* Good grief. Parents were one diaper change away from insanity as it was.

In this new decade, diapers morphed into status symbols. The industry became overrun with a new generation of marketing geniuses. Youngsters not yet of a shaveable age, spewed forth designer diapers with the regularity of Old Faithful. Over-stimulated, creative genes spawned by too much *Sesame Street* began a diaper revolution.

Mothers who once cooed sweetly at babies in the grocery cart could now be seen wild-eyed and drooling in the diaper aisle. This simple purchase of a receptacle for pygmy waste now requires a doctoral degree.

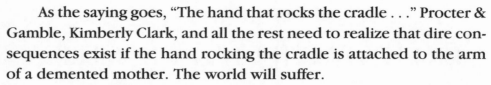

As the saying goes, "The hand that rocks the cradle . . ." Procter & Gamble, Kimberly Clark, and all the rest need to realize that dire consequences exist if the hand rocking the cradle is attached to the arm of a demented mother. The world will suffer.

What began as a minor manufacturing coup led to rumbling revolutions throughout the world. Only those with diapered children were aware of the subtle, slimy changes taking place.

The tentacles of revolution began snaking into all areas of life. Not only were there supermarket scenes of diaper-buying mothers crying in aisles, but new stories surfaced. Stories of people hoping to speedily pick up a simple can of shaving cream, lost for hours searching shelf after shelf for *the* most suitable can of lather. Conversations in this aisle went something like this: "Honey, I need sensitive, face-medium shave for the Miami Vice look with automatic stop-bleed added. Do you see it?"

The revolution moved from diapers and shaving cream to after-school activities for the children. Parents could be heard saying, "The offspring cannot *just* take dance lessons, my dear. They must have an instrument, or better yet, two instruments! They need karate for self-defense; they need football, baseball, soccer, and hockey for sportsmanship. Add to that, piano lessons." Piano lessons used to start for kids about age seven. But now, all Tchaikovsky's began at age two. Professional voice lessons became A Must, as did the after-school Renoir class. To be articulate and accepted, children were told to swim, golf, play tennis, and, oh yes, blow some kind of horn.

All this folderol had not yet reached its limits. Family members began losing track of each other. Pagers were needed to locate children left all over the globe by parents having nervous breakdowns. Cell phones were needed to call home for diaper and shaving cream clarification. Mothers and fathers had to take in freelance work on the weekends to pay for the cell phones, the computers, and the counseling. The counseling was for the children, because they started wetting their pants again. And the counseling was also for the parents, because all this anxiety caused them to start wetting their pants too.

This is how it was. No family was untouched. Mothers and fathers, families, schools, cities, the whole nation, propelled to insanity by too much choice.

The country was ruined. And the blame lies squarely in the wet lap of the diaper kings of the United States.■

—CW

BIRTH OF THE IMAGE BEARER

No book even remotely connected to motherhood would be complete without that coveted Pregnancy, Labor, and Delivery story. Birth stories are God's reward for survival. Women should feel no shame in sharing these stories wherever the mood strikes—at dinner parties, soirees, or diners. This is the stuff of female bonding.

These stories differ from those ever-growing fish tales that men tell. Women don't need to exaggerate labor and delivery stories. They are plenty big and gruesome without embellishment. We share these stories with each other for comfort and . . . to see who wins.

The prize is in two categories: For Ghastliest Pregnancy and Worst Delivery, the prize goes to me. (This is my party, I'll whine if I want to.) I gave drug-free birth to a ten-pound, two-ounce tuna who took one look at the outside world and tried to swim back in. Nothing else needs to be said. I win.

The prize for the second category—For the Weirdest Pregnancy—also belongs to me, for surviving the gestation of my middle child. Like most mothers, I felt I was riding out the lunar months on a raft at high tide. That was not the weird part. The weird part was the host of unpredictable yet ordinary objects precipitating my nausea. And these were things not easily avoidable during activities of daily living.

Mail was a problem. A mere whiff of a harmless pile of mail would bring on a lengthy spell of nausea. I could not unload the post box for the first five months of this pregnancy. To do so would bring on an embarrassing spell of street-side dry heaving. And as any pregnant woman knows, the dry heave trigger is directly wired to the bladder control nerve. An innocuous trip to the mailbox could lead to a socially uncomfortable scene in the presence of one's neighbors.

The next object of my *vomicus automaticus* was hair. A single hair found anywhere it should not be—meaning off the head—gave me projectile vomits. The smell of fabric, the color red, the goldfish, and books bothered me. But the all-time worst offender happened to be decorating magazines. Go figure hormones.

I look at the sweet person God fashioned inside of me and I think, *Why decorating magazines? Why mail? Why thread?* If I were God I would stage a more reverent and solemn beginning for a bearer of my image. A magnificent, holy cloud descending through beams of sunlight perhaps, delivering . . . The Baby, The Image-Bearer. I would not squish up my image inside a vessel the size of a pear, push a bunch of encroaching organs all over the place. I would not top all of that off with a protruding navel. I would not make the carrier of the little Image-Bearer throw up over mail and wet her pants in public. She also would not have gas. It's just not holy somehow.

Go figure God—uncomfortably pedestrian, disturbingly humble, common, simple, and plain. Go figure God—the supreme sculptor—clay in hand, forming a common man to be his son. Go figure God, asking a despised man to be his best friend and a prostitute to

prepare him for death. Go figure God, bridging the hopeless chasm between heaven and earth with a couple of pieces of wood, some nails, and a dead body. Go. Figure God.■

—CW

TEN-DAY-OLD CHARMER

Those who are family to you—those you love most—are the *things most precious.* When it comes time to check out of this old world, you will say, "Bring me my babies, where is my husband? Where are the ones I love? Who cares about *things* and *stuff.*"

One thing most precious to me is my fourth baby. He was ten days old when my Tony (my husband) and I were scheduled to go to a New York festival to lead the festival crowd in praise and worship music. Tony went on ahead in the van. I flew a bit later with the baby.

We arrived at the New York airport and I got on the bus to the festival with a Christian rock band—all the band members had either shaved heads or purple hair. Trollville. This festival week should have been called, How Weird Can I Be? My baby and I were the only normal-looking people there. And it was cold. Real cold. I was shaking. My rings were wobbling. I tried to keep the baby covered and warm.

When it came time for Tony and me to sing, there was no one around—no one, that is, normal-looking enough to hold my baby as I sang.

We were in the community tent where they have colas and juice for all the singers. I said to a teenage girl there, "I have to lead *praise and worship* for communion." I emphasized the *praise and worship,* trying to make it sound like it was a most holy position I had—holier

than anything else. I wanted that girl to think she was holding a most holy infant and she better watch over that baby.

"Could you watch my baby?" I asked.

She said, "Yeah, cool. Sure." She took the baby carrier and plopped my precious baby on a case of colas, on a stack four cases high. My baby was three feet off the ground. I thought, *This will not do for my ten-day-old baby.*

"You know, it's really cold out here," I said.

"I can't leave the stand. I'm serving colas all night long."

"Is there anyone anywhere else who can watch my baby?" I asked.

"Go to the emergency RV."

I thought to myself, *This is emergency enough, chick. I'm outta here.* So I went to the RV. A woman there said, "You have an emergency?"

I said, "Yes, I have a brand new baby. Would you please watch him while I go lead *praise and worship?* " I said it real holy-like again. I handed the woman my baby and I said, "He's brand-new; he's ten days old."

"He'll be all right," she said and plopped him on a table. I turned to go, praying, *Lord, please watch over him.*

I stood up on the stage and as far as my eye could see were kids. After three days of rock-and-roll and weirdness, here were 18,000 teenagers ready to take communion. The minister who was to serve communion explained to us that it would take about thirty minutes to serve the elements. And I thought, *There is no way!—it takes thirty minutes in our little home church to do communion.* He said they were distributing grape juice in little salad-dressing containers with lids. And that they had the wafer bread in a Coke flat.

Then everyone stood up, all 18,000 of them, and they passed around the flat of salad-dressing containers with grape juice and also the bread. As soon as they received the elements, they sat.

From the back of the field, the last one to receive the elements of communion waved, signaling a we-all-have-it-now. The minister blessed the body and the blood. The crowd was silent. They were reverent. There was a holy hush.

Then the minister said, "If any of you would like to make a commitment or if you have made a commitment to Jesus Christ, I would like you to come forward now." I saw them trickle down to the front like in a Billy Graham crusade. I couldn't believe it—in all this humanity and all of this weirdness there were so many who'd made a commitment to God.

We began to sing the chorus, "Our God Is an Awesome God." The kids sang with reverence. The more we sang that song, the more powerful their voices became. They began to roar, *Our God is an awesome God.* . . . They started running in—running in from way back, some smiling, some crying. We must have sung that song fifty times.

I won't forget it as long as I live: The opportunity to serve, and then to be so blessed watching hundreds of kids be perhaps forever changed. I have a saying: What God calls you to, he *graces* you for. That is, what God calls you to do, he gives you strength and the resources to do.

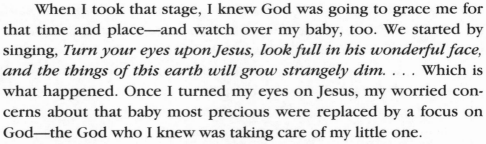

When I took that stage, I knew God was going to grace me for that time and place—and watch over my baby, too. We started by singing, *Turn your eyes upon Jesus, look full in his wonderful face, and the things of this earth will grow strangely dim.* . . . Which is what happened. Once I turned my eyes on Jesus, my worried concerns about that baby most precious were replaced by a focus on God—the God who I knew was taking care of my little one.

When I got back to my baby, he was doing just fine. The woman who was watching over him said he was a perfect little ten-day-old charmer—and a holy child at this blessed event.

The first book of John says, "I set my heart at rest in God's presence." I could have wrestled with the situation, refusing to leave my baby, refusing to worship God. But honest to goodness I was *at rest*. I worshiped, I rejoiced. My God is an awesome God.■

—KB

MOTHER HAIR

I have a well-researched hypothesis about motherhood, hairdos, and ages of children: It is possible to guess very closely the age of a mother's oldest child without ever laying eyes on said child. This is not otherworldly clairvoyance. It is not chemical (like the Draino test pregnant females once took to determine the sex of their child). Anyone can play and become quickly proficient.

The first and only step is to study mom's hairdo. When a first child is born, Mother drops out of life. So consuming is this small, needy mammal that Mama is reduced to a heap of deflated mylar at the end of each day. She's too tired to bathe, much less actually go out in public. Her chic-ness suffers. Years spent meeting Baby's needs translates into less time observing current trends in hair fashion. The poor thing is seen sporting her Birth-of-First-Baby Hair long after the style fell from fashion glory.

Baby eventually grows less dependent on Mama, but another baby comes and then another. When Mama finally reenters the world, she has dinosaur hair—as in *extinct*. Look around. You'll see this is true. Sociologists should study this fascinating theory.

Poor Mama pathetically travels about coifed in the same hairdo as her dropout era. She runs with other Mamas who dropped out with her. They don't know they have Jurassic-era hair as well. Former

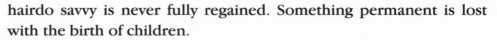

hairdo savvy is never fully regained. Something permanent is lost with the birth of children.

Every so often, however, bad mother-hair can become good mother-hair. This happens if sufficient children are spawned to keep mother out of circulation for a decade or two, in which case the style may recycle and produce good mother-hair. The children go to college and when they come home for Thanksgiving they say, "Gee, Mom, you look so cool now." Everyone thinks the college student has matured enough to notice that Mom isn't really a dork. That's not what's happened at all. She is no cooler now than when she was wearing flood pants at the grocery store when that kid was diapered. Cool never happens again. That hair of hers just cycled around once more.

Here are some quick tips to hair predictions: The seventies mother will probably have shag—Shirley Partridge hair or Carol Bradybunch hair. This is the lucky mother. Her hairdo has risen from the dead and is alive again.

The late-eighties dropout mother will most likely have a lacquered look, much like a helmet. There will be an element of height to it—big, tall hair.

The mom raising babies in the early nineties will have "wall hair." Longer, straight hair. A pouf of curly bangs will be plastered stiff and pointing straight up to heaven. Style note: This was an effective hairdo only when viewed face on. Additional note: This hairdo poses problems when someone sits behind it in the movie theater, as this Great Wall of hairdo is too high to see over.

If you happen to cavort with women who wear finger waves in their hair they will have a seriously old baby. A baby now at least forty-two. A pixie? Her children are from the early sixties.

You see, then, it's really very simple. Not magical at all. You can entertain friends for hours with this theory. There is no end to hair-dos either. Why, you could research it all the way back to Mrs. Neanderthal. She had sprigs, similar to dreadlocks. If you see her children running around, you need to be worried.

If you are a very spiritual type, you might be saying right now, "This is a silly myth. I have learned nothing here." Well, in fact, you *have* learned something. You have actually learned an important piece of Scripture without knowing it. Apostle Paul, that bastion of good advice, said, "Pay no attention to silly myths which give rise to mere speculation." Amen.

—CW

PITFALLS AND ABSURDITIES

Kneeling beside my bed, face buried in the coverlet, I begin to pray. "Lord . . ."

Oldest Baby jams her slobbery thumb into my ear.

"Lord," I begin again, "how am I supposed to become a spiritual giant with a thumb the size of a miniature pickled corn cob stuck in my ear? It's too distracting."

Oldest Baby pulls the slobbery occlusion from my ear. The suction created upon its exit threatens to dislodge the tympanic membrane from residency inside my skull.

"Dear God, I want to be usable, but truthfully, Lord, I've got no *use* left to put an *able* on."

The unmistakable *crinkle, crinkle* of Youngest Baby in his disposable diaper interrupts Middle Baby as she pets my head like a doggie. The small man sporting the diaper then plops down on my calves and uses my praying frame as a chair. He begins to rock in "giddy-up" fashion, wailing loudly when the praying mama "horsy" doesn't respond.

I decide to cry.

God gave me children and then forgot I was still alive, I think. He seemingly dropped me off in this spiritual wasteland called *Motherhood* and forgot to drop back by.

A smart man named Daniel Taylor wrote in his book *The Myth of Certainty*,

> Don't make the mistake of thinking there's another time or another place where following God will come easier. It doesn't work that way. You have everything you need for your contentment or misery within the confines of your own heart. That will go with you wherever you go. Every place has its pitfalls and absurdities, just as each has its opportunities and measures of grace.

How about that?

This place in my life is absurd, all right. Pitfalls abound. So I'm looking for the opportunities and the measures of grace. I'm skeptical though, because Daniel Taylor wasn't a mother.

—CW

DA BIG CHAIR

God will speak to this people, to whom he said, "This is the resting place, let the weary rest"; and "This is the place of repose"—but they would not listen. So then, the word of the Lord to them will become: Do and do, do and do.
—Isaiah 28:11–13, NIV

Jelly globs beckoned me to release them from their incarceration on my table. I picked the path of least resistance across my kitchen floor, hoping to avoid the toddler cookie-drool that threatened to glue me in place. Unmade beds, dirty dishes, unopened bills, carpool responsibilities, the needs of my family—what about my needs?

From the middle of the screaming piles, a small, sweet voice beckoned. I peered over the edge of the basket I was carrying—laundry mounded past my eyebrows.

"Hey, Mom," he said. "Why dontcha come and sit wif me in da big chair?"

Balancing my precarious load, I explained to my toddler, "I have too much to do; I can't sit in the big chair or anywhere else, Honey."

"Come on, come and sit wight here by me." He patted the space between him and the armrest.

"I can't, Baby," I moaned, thinking of the chores that numbered in the legion.

"Come on now; it'll just take a minute, just a wittle minute." He smiled the irresistible smile of a two-year-old boy. He continued to pat the waiting space next to him.

I dropped my load of laundry. I melted into the seat next to him. And he placed his tiny hand on my face, pulled it down to meet his, and said, "Now, isn't dis nice, Mom?"

"Yes," I said, "it's wonderful."

"I sure do wuv you."

"I sure do love you too."

We sat together for a contented, magical ninety seconds.

Then as if he understood the demands waiting for me, he tenderly patted my leg and said, "You can go now."

Just like Jesus. He waits, patting the space next to him and says, "This is the resting place—next to Me."

"Maybe tonight," we say, "maybeafterlunchmaybeafterItakeout thetrashmaybetonightbeforebedmaybetomorrowafterschoolbefore bed." And it doesn't happen.

He keeps patting.

Jesus keeps patting the space between him and the "next thing to do," saying, *Just a little minute. A little minute in My Big Chair. It will change your day, your life.*

"Maybebeforebathtime,bedtime,suppertimemaybemaybe," we drone.

Sit yourself in da big chair. Find your spot in the quiet place. Sit there, so that the Lord doesn't have to say to you, "O.K. then, 'do and do, do and do.'"■

—KB

DISHWASHER SLOP

O nce upon a time, there was only one baby who needed to be fed in my home. This allowed me scads of time to do something about all the worrying and fretting my little brain generated over The Feeding of That Baby. I whipped and pureed myself into a froth over every morsel of food she ingested. Not one microscopic shred of ugly additive or poisonous, processed anything would pass through those rosy little lips, I vowed. Everything from lake trout to bib lettuce was plopped into the food processor, which whirred away many happy hours.

By the time my third child popped on the scene, busyness usurped my allotted frenzy time. I was now too busy to remember if I'd fed the poor kid at all. This concerned him little. *Not a problem,* he would have said if he could talk. This boy gave food the same regard he gave toilet paper—plaything only. My incredible, non-eating boy existed on air.

My husband and I determined that, at eleven months of age, our son was not eating enough to keep a gerbil alive. We were certain he would fall prey to rickets, beriberi, or kwashiorkor (I am a former nurse, and children of former nurses do not get simple ailments). We spent a year's worth of vacation savings on granola bars, cereals, biscuits, pureed anything, fruit jerkys, rice milk, and soy everything. You

name it, we tried it. Solid, liquid, or gas. If the kid ate more than a tablespoon of it, we purchased truckloads of the stuff.

Several months into the baby's anorexia nervosa, I realized he *was* eating something. And he was eating that something with regularity. He was consuming heaps of slop from the open dishwasher door, as well as large food bits dropped by his sisters onto the floor. For a first-time mother this would be a revolting tale. As the parents of multiple children, this was pure comfort.

I was pleased as punch to know he was eating enough to survive infancy and develop a normal brain. Now that the secret to my son's feeding had been discovered, we scattered food around on the floor or scraped it into the dishwasher door as if it were leftovers.

I understand this feeding disorder in my son. It's a genetic thing. I've been known to eat off the floor as I tidy the kitchen. (Embarassing but true.) And I have this problem not only with physical food.

I have a spiritual feeding disorder. Sitting down to a proper meal with my Holy Friend requires a bit of work on my part, and I am usually "too busy." I hunt around for scraps others have left behind after their meal with God. I like my Bible in small leftover crumb bits. A nibble of Romans here, a bite of Isaiah there. I prefer the drive-thru. I want dishwasher slop on the run—even if I know that climbing into my booster seat with a knife and a fork and reading for myself will sustain me longer than the crusts of someone else's interpretation.

I think God knows I can *survive* on the partially digested stuff that is scraped off the plate of some guy who actually read the Bible. But he wants me to get dinner straight from the Chef, served on a china plate. This food is not mixed with everyone else's food. It is not watery. It is pure, unadulterated sustenance.

God, ever the patient parent, sets me a place at his table each day. A knife on the right and fork on the left. He hopes I'm ready to chew. If not, he has been known to fill a sipper cup and set it next to me, happy to see me eating at least enough to sustain life.■

—CW

5

'Possum Served with Cranberry Sauce

Holiday Stories

Holidays are the peculiar occasions of the year where we all decide we need time off. We need time off from work to get the shopping and cooking done. We need time off from dieting so we can enjoy our food. We need time off from mental and physical exertion. And we don't want to do any spiritual growing for a while.

Many people are surprised to learn that God does not take time off for the holidays. He shows up at the diner each day—365 days a year—and prepares our spiritual food. It seems he might even take particular delight in working during holidays. These special days are ripe with opportunities for our soul growth. Why? Mostly because we tend to be more rigid and unyielding about holidays than other days in our year.

We develop a string of absolute rules of how our observances must be, how they must *look. We think to ourselves,* During summer vacation we will be tan and smiling. We will not drown in the sea. At the Christmas dinner table we will look good, eat good food, and spread good will to each other. During spring break we will blah, blah, blah, *and on it goes. Our disappointment*

becomes acute if the real-life day does not turn out like the magazine pictures.

These perfect snapshots secreted away in our minds are what I refer to as the Cranberry Sauces of life. The things that cover up the true food. They are the sauces that cover the main dish—the 'possum, the real world.

God takes delight in working holidays because he works through the froth and anxiety that we whip up in our desire to celebrate (and oh-so-perfectly too) the holidays with those we love. This anxiety is fertile ground for growth—God-style. Any gathering of imperfect people yields diverse opinions and vast opportunities for relational disaster. That's the 'possum. Covering up this unpleasant dish may make for a very pretty picture. But underneath that pretty sauce is a 'possum pure and simple, and it's a food that must be eaten.

This hot plate of anxiety is where God shines as culinary genius. He can turn these troublesome times into the dessert of life if only we trust him. If we can force ourselves to leave the cooking to the Chef and not dash off at the first sign of discomfort, holidays can become the spiritual pièce de résistance of our year.

138

When we are served Holiday 'Possum, we can chomp down that gnarly meat, but it requires a hefty measure of faith and an even greater dose of prayer to accompany it—not just a pretty little cover sauce.

CHINESE EASTER

Sometimes change can be good. Rash changes made to traditional holiday celebrations or meals, however, are usually not-so-good. The rules say, *On Thanksgiving you stay home and eat turkey.* The rules also state, *No one should mess with a family's stuffing recipe.* Simply adding a water chestnut or two to the recipe can inflict all kinds of domestic havoc. The momentary culinary coup is simply not worth the ensuing domestic fallout.

On Christmas Eve, the rule is, *Church is the thing to do before dinner.* And for dinner, *The traditional meal for your family of origin is always the correct one to serve.* (Personally, I've never understood the Italian fish thing for Christmas. It really should be a roast. But to each his own.) The Easter meal *Must also be eaten at home after church.* Though it is not one of the rules, it's best to serve butterflied leg of lamb for Easter. I say *butterflied,* because I once ordered a lamb with the shank in. For reasons I can no longer imagine, I asked the butcher not to shorten the bone. The shank, as a result, would not fit in my oven without a complicated wedging system that left the oven door open all morning.

One year I was forced to change my rigid holiday rules. An overseas trip appeared on my flight-attendant schedule and refused to go away no matter whom I tried to bribe. I was most unhappy. Having

no other choice, I set my dinner table for seventeen and boarded a jet for London. It was the first Easter I spent away from home. Ever.

At six o'clock on this Easter Sunday morning I arrived in London. To snore away the most important day of one's spiritual year in a hotel bed seemed irreverent, so I set out to find a church. I boarded the Tube (the subway train) at Gloucester station, exhausted, almost incoherent, from twenty-eight hours of no sleep.

In my fatigued state I almost stepped into the void between the train and the platform. "Mind the gap," the conductor mumbled without moving his lips.

Having no clear destination, I exited at a station where most of the dressed-up Tube-riders got off, and followed.

We walked west, then north, then east. Around and around we walked until my fatigue gave way to delirium and confusion. The great bells of Westminster Abbey gonged as we rounded the last block. Throngs of Londoners scurried to reach the doors of the famous cathedral.

I couldn't go to Westminster. The Queen Mother might pop in or some other important royal. Embarrassment was too easily available to me in Westminster. I might fall asleep and then drool. I might do something even more hideous.

Surly British bobbies, whose day's assignment was to whisk away errant drooler tourists, would be patrolling if the Windsors were in attendance. I would be that errant tourist. I couldn't risk it. *Manners,* I told myself. *Propriety.*

I am very careful about maintaining English manners because

once, at Harrods (the poshest of department stores), I became faint. I stumbled off discreetly to the corner of a highly polished, marble stairway, successfully avoiding a fall into the £400 caviar basin. As quick as you could say "Jack Sprat," a Harrod bobby-person rushed out of nowhere and said, "Madame, you must not sit on the stair."

"I'm so sorry, but I'm very sick and there was no chair." I became woozy again.

"I'm very sorry, Madame, it is not tolerated." I tried to be a big girl, but I was feeling so bad. I started to cry. The bobby thought this was an even worse scene and became terribly flustered. He escorted me to the ladies lounge, where I had to drop two English pounds to the lounge attendee just to cry where it was tolerated.

Not wishing a repeat of so ghastly a scene, I passed Westminster by. I kept walking and went down a side street named after a proper English gentleman—Nigel or Jeeves or something. There I saw a sign hanging out over the entrance. It said, simply, "Evangelical Church." The door swung out over the sidewalk, which was only as wide as a sausage link. The smallish door opened into an enormous vestibule. The Titanic could have been dry docked right inside that teeny street-side door.

I stopped off at the women's room to splash water on my face and gather my tired wits. A host of Chinese clowns with painted faces and triangle eyebrows bounced in. Some of them appeared to be men. I was uncomfortable with male clowns in my restroom, so I exited, leaving them to do clown things. I went to search out a good seat in the auditorium before the service started.

The enormous sanctuary held fourteen scattered souls, counting me. Without my glasses, the backs of their heads reminded me of early June-peas scattered willy-nilly across the pew backs. The lights dimmed and flickered, casting eerie shadows on the old, stone walls. The place smelled a bit musty and held all the ambiance of Transylvania.

Looking for some instant holiday family, I slid into the same pew as a woman I later learned was from Nigeria. Her turban was as tall as I was, and *she* was taller than any woman I'd ever seen. After some courteous, introductory words, she performed a hard study of her bulletin, ending any chance for further conversation. I'm sure she was afraid of me. My sleep-deprived behavior was beginning to shout: *I am a deranged woman!*

The fourteen of us waited in silence. My head bobbed and jarred in narcoleptic fits resembling naps. I'm certain I snorted and drooled profusely. The Nigerian woman pretended not to notice. When I awoke from one such nap, the room was full.

Hundreds of Chinese people, many of them clowns, had rolled in while I slept. And each one was careful to keep a proper bubble of distance from the others. *The English way,* I thought.

Electric guitars started twanging. The Chinese clowns jumped to their feet and commenced to dancing and jamming—it was as if the chaperone had just left the after-prom party. Pretty soon the whole place was rocking and rolling. I realized why they sat so far from each other: They needed immense personal space for this kind of worship.

I forgot all about the Nigerian woman, the Chinese clowns, and my tiredness. I jammed and danced and worshiped like David in the streets.

A hour or two later the pastor mentioned there would be a Mandarin lunch in the basement with Cokes and a baptism. Everyone was welcome.

I picked up my box of lunch and headed one room deeper into the bowels of Transylvania. In a basement under the "lunch basement," a peculiar music called out to me. The electric guitars tuned and twanged again, mixed now with the Chinese congregation singing Australian songs in accented English.

For the baptism, a crowd gathered around a section covered with white sheets. Sitting in the middle of the sheets was a four-person, rubber life raft. The water-filled raft looked more a long-john doughnut on a doily than a baptismal, but it seemed, in this strange setting, to be just the right thing.

A Chinese man in his forties stepped toward the raft in a white baptismal shift. We all circled around him. He kneeled in the water. All of us watched the man as, emerging from the water, raw emotion washed across his face. For a moment those who surrounded him were privy to an open soul. I wanted to look away, but like everyone else, I was drawn and held by the humility of it all. I started to sob.

After that, the man's frail, eighty-ish mother also came forward in a white shift. She was lifted up into the raft by her sopping-wet, now-crying son. He carried her sideways, like a baby, in his arms. Her head lay against his chest. ***Their two bodies together like that form a kind of cross,*** I thought.

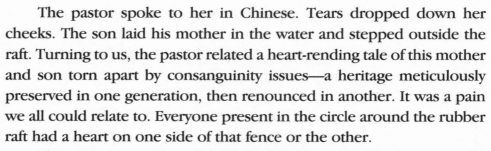

The pastor spoke to her in Chinese. Tears dropped down her cheeks. The son laid his mother in the water and stepped outside the raft. Turning to us, the pastor related a heart-rending tale of this mother and son torn apart by consanguinity issues—a heritage meticulously preserved in one generation, then renounced in another. It was a pain we all could relate to. Everyone present in the circle around the rubber raft had a heart on one side of that fence or the other.

The pastor continued telling the story, explaining that the mother, after seeing the change in her boy, wanted the Jesus who gave her her new son. The soft son. The forgiving son. In the name of Jesus Christ of Nazareth, that pastor baptized the old woman. Those of us who watched felt like we were at the river Jordan. It was holy.

When I heard the story, down in the sheets surrounding that raft I went. Face down. I was wracked with sobs, partially from exhaustion, but mostly from Resurrection feelings.

If God had told me I would spend the most holy Easter of my life with Chinese clowns around a rubber raft, wild hyenas could not have chased me from my home.

Tradition is not a bad thing. Predictability can be comfortable. But I have seen what could be mine when God pried open my hand that Easter weekend and forced me to let go of the familiar.

Change can bring good things—soul-righting things.■

—CW

MOTHER'S DAY FAST

I fast every Mother's day for breakfast. This isn't a spiritual act, because I never *intend* to fast on Mother's day. The day starts like this: Essence of frying bacon travels by scented airwaves to my bedroom. Toast points, all drippy with butter, float around in my imagination like party confetti. I begin to salivate and drool on my pillow like Pavlov's dog.

My children fry, toast, and flip my favorite breakfast food each year, serving me on my special day. They never notice that every Mother's Day for breakfast it's the same—I fast. It isn't that I want to fast. I really want to eat. But the little cooks become so thoroughly famished from their kitchen labors, they forget themselves as they snuggle next to me on the bed. They forget about me, the mom, the honored breakfast guest, and they absently nibble away my repast.

Baggy night shirts hang loose on stick-thin bodies. Wads and tufts of unruly bed hair poke out at right angles from their heads. As the tray is prepared, dirty fists and chewed fingernails push holes into my toast when Dad isn't looking. Anything not too hot to touch is mauled and mutilated almost beyond recognition. By the time the tray is brought to my room, the stuff on the tray is all room temperature and semi-prodded.

Four children and one Dad pile onto the edge of the bed. By now I'm so hungry I almost forget about the fast. But resolve returns, and I

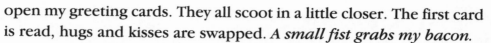

open my greeting cards. They all scoot in a little closer. The first card is read, hugs and kisses are swapped. *A small fist grabs my bacon.*

The family artist fashioned the second card. It has a hole or two where the eraser became overly aggressive in the quest for perfection. The carefully drawn picture is titled "Me and My Mommy." Just the two of us—as if no other members of the family exist. No sister, no brother, no daddy, no dog. Just us two. *My toast is being chewed by the child with the stuffed-up nose. The inside buttery parts are then gnawed out. Only the toast rim remains. Skeletons of toast crusts are left in a pile at the edge of the plate.*

The third card sports a clever saying that makes me laugh. The developing quick-wit of a preadolescent girl gives me pause. She's growing up. How many more Mother's Days will I have her here sitting on my bed? *She drinks my juice.*

I try not to get watery-eyed. They are too young to know that the tears collecting in my eyes are only a little bitter, mostly sweet. For those at this young age, tears are confusing.

A spoonful of cold scrambled eggs remains on the plate. The older ones then discover I've not yet eaten. They chastise the youngest, who starts to cry. Arms swing and defenses are exchanged. Indignant glances are cast in the direction of their father—pleas for intervention.

It's at this point that Mother's Day breakfast is over.

The world cannot boast a four-star restaurant able to lure me. No purchased gift could entice me. The highlight of my year, the finest gift I'll ever receive, is my Mother's Day fast. ∎

—CW

PLASTIC HOLY FAMILY

My friend Annie creates beautiful things. She possesses an amazing sense of loveliness. Every Christmastime it's the same: Her twelve-foot, freshly cut tree fills up with one-of-a-kind crystal and hand-sewn ornaments. Bedecked with ribbons and other assorted pretties, the tree is then topped with sprinkles of dazzling glitter. It sparkles with light. It is spectacular.

Annie hosts a magazine-perfect Christmas—inside the house and out.

But one year, it was different. Deanna, Annie's four-year-old daughter, decided to repeatedly beg for a holy family to be set up in the yard—a whole manger scene constructed outside their home. She wanted the ones that lit up from the inside.

"No," Annie said.

"Why?" her daughter wanted to know.

There were two very good reasons, Annie thought. *Nowhere in this world does an attractive plastic holy family exist.* She told her daughter that no one, anywhere, sold a good-looking "holy family." And the second reason, she said, was that they were plastic. Plastic in the yard would not do. Especially not at Christmas.

These reasons did not satisfy the little girl. She continued to hope that in time she could break Annie's resolve.

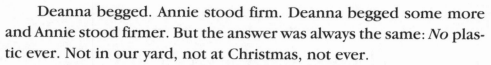

Deanna begged. Annie stood firm. Deanna begged some more and Annie stood firmer. But the answer was always the same: *No* plastic ever. Not in our yard, not at Christmas, not ever.

Then, something changed. Who knows what that something was—perhaps the spirit of Christmas began to sprinkle down from heaven.

The final week before Christmas, the persistence of the four-year-old gained strength and momentum, and the endurance of the mother waned. Annie surrendered.

A late-night trip to Cash Mart limited the possibility of Annie being seen making a *plastic* purchase. To the child's disappointment and the mother's delight, the shelves in the Plastic Holy Family Aisle were empty. "Sold out," said the clerk. Only the display set at the top of the shelf remained.

"Can we buy the holy family from the display area?" Deanna begged.

Stock helpers and a ladder were located. More helpers were summoned to hold the ladder, and even more helpers were needed to hand each individual piece of the life-sized holy family down. The plastic holy family created quite a stir. At ten P.M., Cash Mart had sprung to life.

Annie was in as much agony as her little girl was in bliss.

"One problem," the clerk said. "We don't have boxes for the family since they were display pieces."

Oh, great, Annie thought. *Now we'll have to prop up the plastic people in the cart for all the world to see—one big, happy, plastic family.*

Annie stealthily crept her way to the checkout line, hoping the neighbors wouldn't spot them purchasing the plastic people. Deanna skipped alongside singing,

Away in a manger, no crib for a bed. . . .

Then, of course, the "holy family" was not priced. A price checker needed summoning. Annie, Deanna, and the holy family waited, tying up the line. They waited and then waited some more for a clerk to return with the price.

As she headed through the automatic doors, Annie scanned the parking lot. It was now 11:00 P.M. She was not looking for predators—just making sure no one she knew lurked in the area.

Safely at the car, she opened the trunk to stuff in the bodies. She turned them this way and then that way. But no matter which way she positioned them, the holy family simply did not fit.

"Oh, that's O.K., Mama," Deanna said, "We can just have them ride with us and wear their seat belts. Just like you and me."

Tired and frustrated, Annie strapped Joseph in the front seat and Mary in the back. She went to grab the last piece of plastic, and her daughter said, "I'll hold Jesus, Mama."

Christmas lights sparkled and twinkled as they drove the highway home. Cool, crisp air whispered, *Christmas.*

What's the matter with me? Annie wondered. *Where's the Joy?*

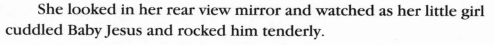

She looked in her rear view mirror and watched as her little girl cuddled Baby Jesus and rocked him tenderly.

. . . no crib for a bed, the little Lord Jesus lay down his sweet head . . .

Annie knew she couldn't see what her daughter saw. She saw only a plastic Jesus, hole in the back of his head and a cord with a Christmas bulb dangling out of it.

. . . Bless all the dear children in thy tender care, and take us to heaven to live with you there.

It was now midnight. Deanna wanted to set the holy family up, on the lawn, lit.

"We cannot go outside now. It's midnight!" said Annie.

"Please, Mama."

"We'll set them up tomorrow."

"Please, then, can we set them up in here?" Deanna asked.

In front of the perfect Christmas tree, they set up the pieces and plugged them in. They were almost done when the little girl ran to her room and brought out a blanket and wrapped Jesus in it. She knelt down near the figures and sang to the plastic Jesus as she placed him gently in the manger.

. . . I love thee Lord Jesus. I ask thee to stay close by me forever and ever, I pray. ■

—KB

QUAIL SHOES

I can never leave well enough alone.

We have wonderful holidays in my family. My sisters, their husbands, my parents, and all our children get together to celebrate. We have glorious times. Memorable moments. But I can never leave well enough alone. *It could always be better,* I think.

Last Thanksgiving I decided that the family needed to be more thankful—they needed to love and appreciate each other more. I should know not to venture into the emotional realm of *thankfulness* and *love* at holiday time, because all that happens is that my general weepy nature turns downright lachrymose at these family gatherings. Sometimes I am weepy, like at last Thanksgiving, because someone I love is sick or in pain. Sometimes I cry simply because I am overwhelmed by how good God has been to me.

Still, here I was at Thanksgiving time venturing into that emotional territory. I fussed for weeks over the Thanksgiving table, hoping to create an atmosphere of thankfulness by my careful attention to detail. Just the *right* plates with just the *right* glasses with just the *right* linens. *Everyone will feel loved and honored,* I thought. An aura of thankfulness would undoubtedly prevail. The carefully prepared ambiance would turn our gluttonous eyes upward to God in thanks for his many gifts.

I composed a short epistle, based on the Bible story of the Exodus,

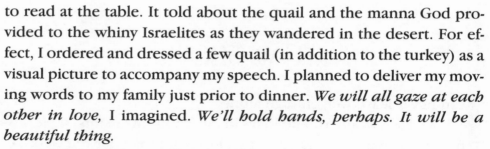

to read at the table. It told about the quail and the manna God provided to the whiny Israelites as they wandered in the desert. For effect, I ordered and dressed a few quail (in addition to the turkey) as a visual picture to accompany my speech. I planned to deliver my moving words to my family just prior to dinner. *We will all gaze at each other in love,* I imagined. *We'll hold hands, perhaps. It will be a beautiful thing.*

I delivered the quail to the table.

"I would like to take a minute to thank God," I said. "We are so blessed—we . . . ha . . . have . . . beautiful, healthy . . . children. . . ." My voice started to crack. "We . . . ha . . . have . . . our health . . . and . . ." I broke into full-blown sobs.

There is nothing pretty about my crying. It comes accompanied by an inordinate amount of uncontrolled blubbering.

No one said a word. Silence draped the air where a moment ago genial conversation and laughter prevailed. My family was so quiet and reverent it was like the pallbearer just closed the casket for the last time. They fidgeted in discomfort as I slobbered on with my racking sobs. My embarrassed preteen's face was the color of diaper rash. Everyone was in pain for me in my humiliating moment. The evidence was on their downturned faces.

Finally, my father cracked, no longer able to squelch the opportunity for a joke. "Oh honey," he said sarcastically, "that was so uplifting." He snickered into his napkin. "I'm blessed. I really am."

With that, they all forgot about me and pitched forks across the table, spearing cold turkey and potatoes.

Later, I surveyed the carnage of the day. Nothing remained intact except the little quail still lying on their spines. Their legs and arms splayed out sideways as if waiting for a diaper change.

Not wanting the little birds to go to waste, my brother-in-law dressed them up with my daughter's pink Barbie doll shoes. I decided, *Well, if you can't preach at 'em, join 'em,* so I helped him figure out a way to fasten tutus to the birds' oven-roasted skin. We carefully prepared them to go into my other brother-in-law's lunch.

My embarrassing social gaffe was forced into everyone's Bad Memories File—the way people stuff memories of motion sickness from car rides or the passing of kidney stones. I did not succeed at making the holiday a more thankful one. But then, it wasn't necessary to make us more thankful. We are already a grateful people. My family is not the sort to forget God on any day, much less a holiday.

Well, maybe they were a *bit* more thankful: They were thankful to realize that a whole month would exist before I could over-spiritualize and over-blubber at the next family holiday gathering. ■

—CW

GETTING IT

For days he kept asking, "How much longer till the play about Jesus, Mom? Three more days, Mom? How many days is three, Mom? Is it before Easter or after Easter, Mom?"

Finally the big day arrived. We took our seats on the aisle in the balcony. His toddler legs, not much longer than stumpy potato tubers, poked straight out to the end of his seat. His four-inch, hang-down tie shifted sideways from under his collar and came to rest just under his left ear. He waited, mustering all the patience he'd accrued in his four years on earth.

His breathing clipped with anticipation as the lights dimmed. His pupils grew large. He squirmed, looking stage left, stage right. "Where is he, Mommy? I can't see him." *How neat*, I thought. *He's looking for Jesus.*

The imaginative stage settings, the bright lights, even the pyrotechnics held little appeal for Gregory. He was looking for the Son of God. I was so proud of his spiritual depth at just age four.

The final weeks of the life of Christ played out on the stage below. Greg scooted to the edge of his seat. A Roman soldier, bedecked in all the soldier finery of the day, moved in to seize Jesus. Thick, burnished armor covered the warrior. Something like a whiskbroom, dyed red, arched across his helmet. The soldier and his comrades dragged, shoved, thorn-crowned, and nailed Jesus to the cross.

I watched Greg's face in the light provided by the grand finale, the resurrection explosion.

He's got it, I thought. *He sees what Easter is all about. It's not about a rabbit or eggs, it's about a Savior.*

Greg's eyes darted back and forth, up and down, searching to imprint every detail for later recall.

The lights rose. And the drama playing out before us came to a close. I picked up my son to expedite our descent from the balcony seats. "What did you think of the play, honey?" I asked rather loudly. Secretly I hoped the surrounding patrons would hear his inspired answer.

"Oh, Mom, I really wish I could be the soldier that put Jesus on the crust."

Greg didn't get it at all. He missed the savior point. He fell for the glitz of the soldier garb. He fell for the red whiskbroom. He missed seeing power in the plain-looking, half-clothed man being nailed to a piece of wood. He missed the point about the savior that no one could keep in a grave.

I guess I don't really get it either. The Savior thing. The nails, the blood. The plain man who says he whispered my name as the soldier hammered him to the cross. I don't get it. It seems so gruesome, so messy.

I am not drawn to gruesome and messy. I am drawn to *tidy* and *nice,* to *pretty* and *clean.* I don't get it. But that's not the point really. Gregory and I don't have to get it. We just have to say "yes" to it—to accept it. We simply have to stop trying to figure it out—stop trying to

sift the Cross through our human minds and spit it back out in our limited human verbiage.

The Cross is the holiest of dramas written by God. It was his finest hour. Maybe it wasn't meant to be understood. Just accepted.■

—CW

VACATION-SINKING SPIRIT

After weeks of planning, of drooling over brochures that offered The Finest Holiday Vacation Package Ever, here I was away from real life. No job. No kids. No phone. Nothing but fun, fair weather, and relaxation. I swung in a hammock and sipped from a cute, umbrella-straw stuck into a coconut. Little did I know I would almost drown on this, the third day of my cruise.

As the snorkeling instructor listed important safety precautions, I only half-listened. I couldn't wait for him to finish telling the rules so I could get out there. In the faded, orange vest and huge flippers, I looked like an eager, overdressed buoy.

Finally he finished talking. We waded out into the deep. We were all facedown in the water, bobbing up like popcorn in our excitement. It wasn't long before my too-big, borrowed fins filled with water and became too cumbersome to be of any use. I quickly tossed them to the shore, not wanting to be weighed down and miss any fun.

Several times I came up for air before I realized that no one was near me anymore. I was further out than I had realized.

I began heading for shore. The more I pressed toward shore, though, the more the current pulled me back. I knew the rule was to swim diagonally across the current until I could swim out of it. But

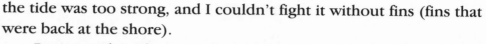

the tide was too strong, and I couldn't fight it without fins (fins that were back at the shore).

Panic enveloped me. Salt water was all I could see. All I could feel and touch was salt water. Salt water everywhere and no way out. I was in a water coffin. The vest bobbed, pulling up around my neck, irritating me instead of helping me. Strange thoughts floated into my head. *This is it. I'm tired of trying. I'm going to let this vest go and slip into the deep. I'm going to drown.*

My panic times came, as most people's panic times do, mingled with pleas to God: "Help, Lord. I'm the little woman in the Atlantic Ocean in a big orange life vest; you can't miss me. Help. Help me not be afraid. Help me not lose my mind." As soon as my brain clamped onto prayer rather than panic, determination filled my sinking spirit. *I have a life vest on. What am I thinking? I can tread water for days if I have to.* I tightened the straps on my vest. I prayed again, more determined, "God, give me clear thinking. Don't let me lose hope."

Then I remembered the instructor's words, "Don't go beyond the perimeter."

Perimeter. If there is a perimeter, then it must be marked off somehow. I turned around and looked. Several yards further out I found marking ropes.

Hand over hand, I pulled myself in.

An amazing thing happened: Once I realized I had the rope, I even began to enjoy the "pull" back to shore. It took me nearly two hours. As I pulled, with my snorkle and mask I looked on the underside of the water and saw God's spectacular underwater creations. I was where no man had dared to go. But I wasn't alone. ■

—KB

OF CHRISTMAS ANGST AND ANGELS

It was Christmastime. I felt it rising. The tide of frustration was rising. I wanted to scream something, and it was not "HO, HO, HO." I hated everything—this strip mall, the town, my house, the traffic, the weather, my hair, my life.

The stores were predictably crowded. The crowd predictably short-tempered. I forged paths through the clusters of bodies, tugging my two small girls behind me. I tried to avoid the Christmas Train that circled around Santa and his battalion of silly elves. I hoped to avoid the jangly bells because I already had jangly nerves, but the force of the crowd propelled us toward the lacquered train and all its Styrofoam decorations.

"Can we please, Mommy? Please? Please, can we ride?"

"I'm sorry, no," I said flatly. "I don't have any money."

I did have money, but I was too tired to fish it out of my purse. I didn't want to wait for sixty-five toddlers to ride the train in a dizzying circle before mine got on. I didn't want to stand even one minute squashed between sticky little Benny and his Aunt Emma. I wasn't out of money, I was out of patience and precariously close to being out of my mind.

A young, thirty-ish man stood alone next to us, watching the circling train without emotion. I wondered why on earth he was here. He seemed not to be waiting for anyone to get off the Christmas

Train. He was unencumbered by packages and apparently not planning to shop, as the mall was closing soon. This was the last place I'd be standing if I didn't have to be.

I tugged at the hands of my now silent and disappointed little girls and turned to cut a path through the crowd. Just as we were heading away, the young man grabbed my hand and pressed a dollar into it. Without looking at me or showing any emotion, he said, "Please give them a ride."

"Oh, I couldn't—" I began to protest. "I have money. I just—" I opened my purse and reached in for my wallet. In that second, he vanished. Somehow, he slipped through the thickness of the crowd without a sound. Vanished. The crowd swelled into the spot he once occupied.

My girls rode that Christmas Train, pink-cheeked and screeching with delight. Fifty cents a piece to see those smiles. A little bit of heaven in those smiles.

For the grand sum of one dollar, one regular mom purchased a sliver of God, thanks to a stranger.■

—CW

How Your love is unfailing
  Your mercies are new
How Your blessings pour out on us
  Our strength is renewed
How we're drawn a little closer
  When we talk about You.

—KB